LINCOLN CHRISTIAN COLLEGE

P9-CFK-186

LINCOLN CHRISTIAN COLLEGE AND SEMINARY

STOP SETTING GOALS

If You
Would
Rather
Solve
Problems

STOP
SETTING
GOALS

If You
___
Would
___
Rather
___
Solve
___
Problems

Bobb Biehl

President of Masterplanning
Group, International

MOORINGS
Nashville, Tennessee
A Division of The Ballantine Publishing Group, Random House, Inc.

STOP SETTING GOALS IF YOU WOULD RATHER
SOLVE PROBLEMS

Copyright © 1995 by Bobb Biehl

All rights reserved under International and Pan-American Copyright
Conventions. Published in the United States by Moorings, a division of
the Ballantine Publishing Group, Random House, Inc., New York, and
simultaneously in Canada by Random House of Canada Limited,
Toronto.

Scripture taken from the HOLY BIBLE, NEW INTERNATIONAL
VERSION®. NIV®. Copyright © 1973, 1978, 1984 by International
Bible Society. Used by permission of Zondervan Publishing House. All
rights reserved.

Library of Congress Cataloging-in-Publication Data

Biehl, Bobb.
    Stop setting goals if you would rather solve problems / Bobb
Biehl. — 1st ed.
        p.   cm.
    Includes bibliographical references (p.   ).
    ISBN: 0-345-39566-2 (hard)
    1. Problem solving.   2. Goal setting in personnel management.
I. Title.
HD30.29.B5   1995
658.3—dc20
                                                        95-18125
                                                        CIP

First Edition: June 1995

10   9   8   7   6   5   4   3   2   1

Contents

112332

CONTENTS

**Part Two: Primary Benefits of the
Stop Setting Goals Model**

**Part Three: Team Implications of the
Stop Setting Goals Model**

CONTENTS

Acknowledgments

A special thank you to Cheryl Biehl, my wife, whose love has been basic to all my goal setting and problem solving. Thank you, Cheryl.

A special thank you to Dr. Mary Beshear, my editorial associate, whose support was invaluable. Thank you, Mary.

A special thank you to Ross Goebel, my executive assistant, without whom this book would not be in your hands. Thank you, Ross.

A special thank you to Bill Needham, my lifelong friend, whose research has added dimension to my work over the years. Thank you, Bill.

A special thank you to Claude Robold, my friend and president of Mentoring Today, whose thoughts have added a great deal to the strength of this book. Thank you, Claude.

A special thank you to Elliott Snuggs, a client and friend, whose editorial notes from a problem solver's perspective have proven invaluable.

Introduction

Would you rather reach goals or solve problems?

If you are one of the millions of men and women worldwide who prefer solving problems to setting goals (my estimate is that from 60 percent to 90 percent of the world's population prefer problem solving to goal setting), just the word *goals* puts a small knot in the pit of your stomach.

If you are a problem solver, this book was written for you!

I had been teaching goal setting for more than twenty years when one morning I had a "eureka!"-type of revelation I hadn't expected at all. I was working with an executive team of about ten vice presidents at Dave Ray and Associates in Troy, Michigan (the Detroit area). Dave Ray and Associates is an electronics firm specializing in sophisticated electronic technology, gauges, guidance systems, and the like. The executive team members are mostly engineers and sales personnel. I asked each member of the group, "What is your *single greatest strength?* What do you *do* the very best?"

Since sharing personal strengths is not usually an embarrassing exercise, I went around the circle and asked each person to tell the group his or her single greatest strength so the others in the group could call for help in that specialty area. *Innocent and simple enough.* Or so I thought. I don't know what it was about that morning but it was as though each person had been divinely appointed to teach me a truly profound lesson that had escaped my observation for more than twenty years.

When sharing with the group what they saw as their strength, half of the team members said, in effect, "My strength is reaching goals."

The other half said, "My strength is solving problems."

There was no comparing of notes beforehand, but it was as though I needed that "live" object lesson to come to the realization that some people naturally see their entire world through the lens of goals and other people naturally see their entire world through the lens of problems.

EUREKA!
OF COURSE!
HOW COULD I HAVE BEEN SO DENSE?
NO WONDER!
AHA!

It was as though, in one fraction of a second of insight, twenty years of frustration (trying to teach goal setting to problem solvers) made complete, 100 percent sense.

These problem solvers were not dense (not unable to grasp goal setting). It was I who was dense (not truly understanding problem solvers). This one insight gave me new eyes. It helped me to learn hundreds of lessons about goal setters and problem solvers since that life-changing morning.

One such profound lesson came one morning shortly thereafter, when I was working with Josh McDowell, who has spoken live to millions of college students, has written many best-selling books, has his own television program, and has over a dozen different video titles.

I was teaching his executive team what we call our "Executive Leadership Program." In this program, we spend two days a quarter for two years with the vice-presidential-level members of a staff, teaching them to think like presidents. One morning I gave a lecture on "Stop Setting Goals." Afterward Bob Nickol, the bright thirty-eight-year-old director of operations, came up to me. He shocked me with this simple comment:

"This has been one of the freest days of my life."

Looking at him with a puzzled expression, I asked him to explain, to expand, and to help me understand what he meant. He said, "I have hated setting goals ever since I can remember, but *I love solving problems*. Every time someone asks (or insists) that I set goals, my stomach goes into knots. I get irritable, cranky, kick at the proverbial dog, and generally become miserable to live with around the house. When I am forced to set goals, I find myself wanting to *come to work late and leave early,* not to mention the lack of natural motivation and energy I have in the six to twelve hours I do spend here, grinding it out. But if I could define my work as solving problems rather than setting goals, I would *come in early and leave late!*"

That morning one question nearly overwhelmed me: "How many millions of times a day is this story repeated around the world? How much energy is lost because problem solvers are stuck on goal-setting teams? How many multiplied millions or even billions of dollars are wasted daily because de-motivated problem solvers are forced to set goals?" That was the morning that writing this book became a specific, measurable, short-range priority!

Problem solvers frequently feel like second-class citizens in the shadow of goal setters and the pervasive goal-setting orientation that has become standard in so many corporate cultures and even in many national cultures.

"I no longer feel like a second-class citizen" is easily the statement most frequently made by individuals after they hear a lecture on "Stop Setting Goals." It is not just a phrase coined for this book. That actual statement has come word for word literally tens if not hundreds of times from the lips and hearts of people who feel a new kind of freedom after they hear the idea.

Problem solvers are not second-class citizens. They are the defensive unit of the team that complements the offensive unit (goal setters). Both goal setters and problem solvers are absolutely indispensable whenever you want to win the games of life!

Do you feel energized by goals and drained by problems? Or do you feel energized by problems and drained by goals?

If you can identify whether you are a goal setter or a

problem solver and work within your preference, you and any team you lead will experience:

- maximized natural energy;
- reduced anxiety, conflict, and tension;
- increased productivity;
- increased team spirit, morale, and respect;
- improved communication;
- increased confidence; and
- increased efficiency and competitiveness.

The implications of letting goal setters set goals and problem solvers solve problems are huge for all teams. Consider the implications of the benefits just listed for:

- a major computer company's executive team,
- the office staff of a local high-school principal,
- the staff of a governor, senator, or representative, or
- a professional sports team,
- any team on which you choose to play—*your* team!

THE IMPORTANCE OF PROBLEM SOLVING

Over the years, I have frequently counseled people who wanted better jobs to show more initiative . . . to develop an effective presentation showing how their abilities can help solve the organization's problem. It's called "solution selling," and is a key paradigm in business success.

But people who end up with the good jobs are the proactive ones who are solutions to problems, not problems themselves, who seize the initiative to do whatever is nec-

essary, consistent with correct principles, to get the job done.
Stephen R. Covey in The Seven Habits of Highly Effective People:
Restoring the Character Ethic[1]

A few personal notes as you read this book: As you read my biographical sketch on the dust jacket of this book, you may get the impression that Bobb Biehl is a theoretical person who writes books from an ivory tower, disconnected from day-to-day realities of the workplace. That is not so. Since 1976 I have made my living consulting with clients around the world, day after day after day. The practical material in this book was born in extremely candid conversations with these clients, not in a dark, dusty, isolated ivory tower.

I did not grow up attending private schools and being chauffeured to school in a long, shiny, black limousine. I grew up working on turkey farms with my grandparents, aunts, uncles, and cousins near a rural village called Mancelona, Michigan. A lot of what you read in this book is plain old turkey-farm logic.

My family has always valued common sense. My dad, Bob Biehl, has many sayings, principles, and rules of thumb he calls *nutshells*. A nutshell is a kernel of truth, the essence, or the heart of the matter. That is the kind of insight you will find in this book. This book will be as practical as I can make it. No big words. No complicated theories. What you find here is just what has been tested in the real world of my consulting practice, worldwide, with clients in large and growing churches, nonprofit organizations, and for-profit corporations.

The entire book is written to be "tomorrow morning

practical," whether you work with a Fortune 500 company, a mom-and-pop start-up business, a local high school, an architectural firm, or a government office. In fact, I want it to be practical for you *every* morning, no matter where you go or what you do for the rest of your life.

I have written this book imagining that you are a person who loves solving problems and we are sitting on the boardwalk at Main Beach in Laguna Beach, California, or on the white sand and crushed coral two miles south of Flagler Beach, Florida (two of my favorite ocean spots). We would just chat about life and share insights about people that would help you know how to get "round pegs into round holes." The following pages contain what I would tell you if we were to sit watching the water and just talk about goals . . . problems . . . people . . . and how to make it in life. This material is designed to help you grow in your understanding—first of yourself, and then of other people.

Even though mentoring cannot take place at a distance, this book has been written in a mentoring, how-can-I-help-you-win? style. The insights offered will give you new eyes to see how people differ and new confidence to believe that it's okay to be who you are and let others be who they are.

One last introductory thought: Whenever the word *team* is used, it means any team—your work team, your sports team, your volunteer team, or your family team. *Team* in this book simply means a group of people working together to reach a commonly desired end. You may be part of more teams than you first think. You may be on a board of elders at church, a softball team at work, a family reunion planning team for the family, and many others.

The heart of this book is a promise to you. When your team is defined so that your goal setters are playing offense and your problem solvers are playing defense, your team will be much much stronger! When you, as a problem solver, are totally free to solve problems and the goal setters on your team are just as free to set goals, your team will play better, have more energy, or be more productive. Helping you make the transition successfully is what this book is all about.

PART ONE

Personal Implications of the Stop Setting Goals Model

1

Do You Feel Energized by Goals or by Problems?

How honest can you be with yourself? We each have three selves:

1. First, we each have a *public self* that everyone sees. This is our image, our package, our front, our smile, and our mask.
2. Second, we each have a *private self* that only close friends and family see in private situations. It's a little less guarded, a little more open, a little more revealing, and a little less cautious. We will tell our close, good, wonderful friends things in private that we would never say in public.
3. Third, we each have a *personal self* that only we have ever seen. Even our closest friends have not seen this part of us. This is our heart, the real you and the real me. This is our heartbeat, the part of us that only we know.

No matter how close we are to any friend, including a spouse, there are certain things in our hearts that we have never told anyone.

So I ask you again, in your heart of hearts, where no one else sees, regardless of what your father or mother preferred, regardless of what your team expects of you, regardless of what you think you should or ought to enjoy most, which of these processes *energizes* you the most?

☐ **Setting goals and reaching them, or**
☐ **Defining problems and solving them?**

A clarification might be helpful. *Goal setting* is adding totally new dimensions to the existing system (program, idea, project). *Problem solving* is solving the problems within the existing system (program, idea, project). For example:

CONTEXT	GOALS	SOLUTIONS
Home construction and repair	Build a new house or add a room to the existing house	Repair the wiring in the existing house or replace the carpet
Publishing	Write a book	Edit a book
Computers	Add a new computer or develop a new program	Fix a problem in the existing computer or simply add memory

Automobiles	Buy a new car	Fix up the old car for another year
Marketing	Take on a new line of products	Improve profitability of the existing line
Education	Change the curriculum that was taught last year to something new	Improve or refine the way the curriculum was taught last year
Coaching	Score x points	Keep the opposing team from scoring points
Food preparation	Create entirely new recipes	Improve proven recipes
SUMMARY	**ADD NEW DIMENSIONS TO THE EXISTING SYSTEM!**	**SOLVE THE PROBLEMS WITHIN THE EXISTING SYSTEM!**

INVENTORY: A PATH TO SELF-DISCOVERY AND UNLOCKING YOUR NATURAL ENERGY LEVEL

Whenever I speak on Stop Setting Goals, about twenty-five minutes into the lecture, I typically pause and ask how many in the audience have a crystal clear understanding of which they prefer, setting goals and reaching them or defining problems and solving them. Typically 70 percent to 80 percent of the audience members raise their hands, indicating that they know clearly whether they prefer working on goals or problems. The remaining 20 percent to 30 percent ask for a little more explanation and possibly an inventory to help them decide.

At several points in the book you will find an inventory, a series of questions, or a profile to help you explore a self-defining trail that will help you distinguish things you like and don't like, things you prefer to do and prefer not to do. The following is an inventory to help you know if, in your heart of hearts, you prefer setting goals and reaching them or defining problems and solving them.

This is not a test! It is an inventory. You cannot pass or fail. This is simply a look at which you prefer —goal setting or problem solving.

Please read each of the ten questions and place a check in the GOALS box or the PROBLEMS box for each of the ten questions. When you have finished, add the number of checks to identify your preference. It is perfectly OK to have a check or two that is not consistent with the other checks.

QUESTION	GOALS	PROBLEMS
1. Which word have you used most in casual conversation and thought about excitedly in the past six months?		
2. Which word gets you excited, motivated, energized?		
3. Which word does *not* leave you feeling drained, de-motivated, and de-energized?		
4. In a new situation, does your mind naturally start searching for goals or for problems?		
5. In games or sports, do you most enjoy the offensive plays and strategy (check GOALS) or the defensive plays and strategy (check PROBLEMS)?		

6. If you had your choice for the next year, would you plan your work by setting goals and reaching them or by defining problems and solving them?		
7. Would you prefer to add new parts to an existing system (check GOALS) or to fix an existing system (check PROBLEMS)?		
8. Would you prefer to lead a team in reaching a goal or in solving a problem?		
9. Which gives you less stress, pressure, and anxiety: setting and reaching goals or defining and solving problems?		

10. Think back to your fourth-grade playground. instinctively, did you most enjoy scoring points (check GOALS) or keeping others from scoring points (check PROBLEMS)?		
TOTAL NUMBER CHECKED		

A few clarifying notes on the numbered questions in the inventory above:

#1. Goal setters talk a lot about goals, and problem solvers talk a lot about problems. Look at which you talk about most, and you'll get an idea of which you naturally prefer.

GOAL SETTERS TALK ABOUT	PROBLEM SOLVERS TALK ABOUT
Goals and dreams	Problems and realities
New hills to climb	Following through on the commitments already made . . . last year
New challenges	Maximizing and controlling
Golden opportunities	Roadblocks

#2. Just mentioning the word *goals* is exciting to goal setters. Their eyes focus, their hearts beat just a bit faster, and their ears listen with a little more intensity. On the other hand, just mentioning the word *problems* is exciting to problem solvers. Their eyes focus, their hearts beat just a bit faster, and their ears listen with a little more intensity.

#3. Just hearing the word *goals,* much less working on goals, tends to drain problem solvers' energy. The excitement leaves their hearts, and they feel tired, fatigued, exhausted, spent, done.

Exactly the opposite is true with the goal setter. Just hearing the word *problems,* much less solving problems, tends to drain goal setters' energy. The excitement leaves their hearts, and they feel tired, fatigued, exhausted, spent, done.

#4. Goal setters are oriented in a new situation by goals. They keep asking, "Where are we going?" "What is our direction?" "How do we take full advantage of this window of opportunity?" "What are our goals?"

Problem solvers are oriented by problems. In a new situation, problem solvers ask, "What is wrong?" "What's broken?" "How do we fix it?"

#5. Goal setters tend to enjoy (whether watching or playing) offensive strategy, regardless of their game or sport of choice. Problem solvers tend to enjoy defensive strategy. Which do you enjoy most? You may have played both offense and defense in your school days because you were skilled at both, but the one you instinctively enjoyed the most is the one you will watch or play with the most interest today.

GOAL SETTERS TEND TO BE MORE INTERESTED IN	PROBLEM SOLVERS TEND TO BE MORE INTERESTED IN
The backfield and touchdowns	The defensive unit and sacks
The batter	The pitcher and key defensive players
Points scored	Keeping the other team from scoring
Principle: The best defense is a strong offense	Principle: The best offense is a strong defense

#6. As you look forward to the next year, which would you do if you had a choice: set goals and reach them or define problems and solve them? When you think about the next year or the next ninety days, do you instinctively start thinking of new goals you will reach? Or do you think of problems that need to be solved first? When you get out your personal planner, do you make lists of goals to be reached or problems to be solved? What you do naturally (or wish you could do) is a leading indicator of your instinctive energizers —goals or problems.

#7. Goal setters continually want to add new dimensions to the existing system, program, or organization. Problem solvers prefer to refine, maximize, and improve the existing system, program, or organization.

GOAL SETTERS WANT TO	PROBLEM SOLVERS WANT TO
Get a new car	Fix up the old car
Build a new wing on the building	Improve the lighting in the existing building
Start a new business	Maximize the business currently owned
Get new customers	Serve existing customers better

#8. Frequently, by leading a team we are able to see clearly whether we prefer goal setting or problem solving. Would you prefer to lead a team in scoring points? Or would you prefer to lead a team in holding the other team to zero points?

#9. Goal setters actually feel very little stress in the goal-setting and goal-reaching processes, whereas problem solvers frequently experience a great deal of stress in these processes. Problem solvers experience very little stress when defining problems and solving them, whereas goal setters frequently experience high blood pressure when even thinking about having to deal with ongoing problems.

GOAL SETTERS TEND TO	PROBLEM SOLVERS TEND TO
Be more open to moving to a new house	Avoid the topic of moving as long as possible
Want to add new rooms	Want to fix up and remodel
Buy new things and discard old things	Fix and keep old things, which they consider as good as new
Spend money freely (not unwisely)	Save for a rainy day

#10. I've talked with hundreds of men and women about their fourth-grade playground experiences. Most of them can remember that by the fourth grade (approximately nine to ten years old), they instinctively enjoyed either scoring points (goal setters as adults) and/or keeping others from scoring points (problem solvers as adults). The correlation between our fourth-grade behavioral patterns and our adult preferences for goal setting or problem solving is absolutely amazing to me.

If you are still unsure which activity you prefer, you might find creating the following profile for yourself helpful.

MY SELF-PORTRAIT

On each row, check the box on the left or the right that most nearly reflects your thoughts, feelings, or preferences.

GOAL SETTERS' STRENGTHS	PROBLEM SOLVERS' STRENGTHS
☐ I love setting goals, and it is emotionally very satisfying every time I reach a goal I have set.	☐ I love solving problems, and it is very emotionally satisfying every time I solve a problem no one else could solve.
☐ I keep going over my goals. I keep track of the big picture, possibly forgetting problems.	☐ I lose track of or forget goals, but I keep tightly focused on problems.
☐ Most people think of me as an extremely positive and optimistic goal setter, although I appear to some as unrealistic.	☐ I see myself as an extremely positive and optimistic problem solver, although some people misread me and think of me as negative.
☐ I am basically a risk taker once the goal is clearly defined.	☐ I will take some risks, but only after careful research has been completed and the potential problems have been carefully identified.

☐ I am continually seeking a new and different goal.	☐ I tend to stay with the tried and true, the proven, solid successes.
☐ I find a clearly defined goal energizing.	☐ I find a good, hard problem energizing.
☐ I am "hard to guard" when going for one of life's "goal lines" to score points.	☐ No one gets around me. I can ask enough tough questions to stop poorly developed ideas.
☐ I identify more with the Marines: Bomb the bridge and take the beachhead!	☐ I identify more with the Army Corps of Engineers: Rebuild the bombed-out bridge and reconstruct the beach.
☐ I go for the gold!	☐ I go for the gold— after I make sure we don't lose the gold we already have!

GOAL SETTERS' STRUGGLES	PROBLEM SOLVERS' STRUGGLES
☐ I sometimes have trouble seeing and dealing with obvious problems and being patient with all the seemingly negative questions problem solvers ask.	☐ Sometimes I find it difficult to keep the big picture in view. I tend to get lost in the details of a project or a problem.

☐ I get bored rather easily and constantly need new goals to keep me challenged.	☐ I am somewhat uncomfortable with new goals, especially where there are no proven models or in situations I have never seen before.
☐ I dislike and tend to put off detailed follow-through and prefer heading toward my next big goal.	☐ I frequently find it difficult to face new situations. I distrust my own instincts when I am in a new situation.

TYPE OF SUPERVISION GOAL SETTERS PREFER	TYPE OF SUPERVISION PROBLEM SOLVERS PREFER
☐ I really need to have clear goals and to be given the resources and the freedom to reach them.	☐ I prefer to be assigned specific problems that have stumped everyone else for some time and then solve them.
☐ I need to keep my goals visible and constantly carry with me a list of the goals I am working on.	☐ I keep a list of problems with me all of the time and look at them frequently throughout the week.
☐ I celebrate goals reached far more than I do problems solved.	☐ I celebrate problems solved far more than I do goals reached.

THE QUESTION THAT'S USUALLY IN MY MIND WHEN I'M AROUND PROBLEM SOLVERS	THE QUESTION THAT'S USUALLY IN MY MIND WHEN I'M AROUND GOAL SETTERS
☐ "Why are you always so negative?"	☐ "Why set new goals when you didn't follow through on the ones you set last year?"

TOTAL POINTS: ___ Goal Setter ___ Problem Solver

BOTTOM LINE, I AM BASICALLY A: _____

MATURE SENIOR EXECUTIVE: A PROBLEM SOLVER

Recently I had the occasion to explain Stop Setting Goals to a longtime friend and client, Dr. Robert Lewis, the teaching pastor of a church with approximately four thousand members, a writer, and a national speaker on family issues.

During lunch, I sketched out the Stop Setting Goals concept for him. At the end, I asked him, "Do you prefer setting goals or solving problems?"

His response intrigued me. He said, "Well, I think of what you are saying in terms of football. I made the all-state football team in high school on both offense and defense, so it's a little bit hard for me to say which I like best. I guess I have never really thought about it in just those terms. Let me think about it for a minute."

There was a twenty- to thirty-second pause. Then, recalling his days as a teeth-loosening, line-crushing, hel-met-cracking all-state middle linebacker, he smiled broadly and said with the greatest of clarity and confidence:

"I loved tackling people!"

He continued with the confidence of a mature senior executive: "Today I am basically a problem solver, a defensive captain. I really get energized to lead a group against a problem that needs to be held in check and corrected." He said, "That's when I really find my leadership at its best. That's when I really enjoy mobilizing people!"

2

It's OK to Be Who You Are

What are the implications in your personal work of spending hundreds and thousands of hours, over the next ten years or so, working in a position that is the exact opposite of what you really want to do, what you most enjoy, and what you do best?

As a problem solver, try to imagine a world in which you go to work, and the minute you get to work your team leader is talking about, cheering about, and holding you accountable for the big G—GOALS! Now imagine the pleasure of going to work each day and your assignment is to solve a problem no one else has been able to solve!

Or imagine the amount of wasted, grind-it-out, make-yourself-do-it, forced energy that your goal-setter friends at work would spend if every day they went to work and all of the assignments required solving problem after problem after problem and never let them focus on fresh, new, energizing goals for the future. Now imagine the freedom your friends would experience, as goal setters, to be able to go to work and to concentrate primarily on goals.

As much as possible, work with your natural instincts, not against them, and help everyone you know to do the same.

Do this even if your preference is different from every member of your family for generations.

Do not try to be someone you are not. It will cause you great stress and deep frustration.

You may be in a position today where you have no choice. You may be stuck in a job where you have to go outside of all that is comfortable to you and live with Winston Churchill's assessment of reality:

"Sometimes our best is not enough, we must do what is required!"

If you are in this position, begin looking, as soon as possible, for a way to adjust your current work environment. If it is just not adjustable, begin looking, as soon as possible, for alternative job possibilities. (See the Career Change Questions in Appendix B.)

Our grandparents and parents (especially those who went through the Great Depression in the late 1920s and early 1930s, as well as those who lost their "secure" positions with the downsizing or rightsizing of corporations in the 1980s and those laid off permanently during economic cycles known as recessions in the past twenty-five years) lived (or live) life thankful just to have a steady job, a paycheck they could count on, bread on the table, and the wolf away from the door!

Today, most people are not looking for just a job. They are looking for ways to maximize themselves. Ways to fulfill their destinies. Ways to find personal fulfillment. Ways to make a living in a life style they enjoy!

From my experience, I would estimate that 60 percent to 70 percent of the people you and I deal with on a day-to-day basis are somewhere between only mildly satisfied with their current work to very deeply dissatisfied with it. One of the main reasons is that there are so many goal setters in problem-solving positions and problem solvers in goal-setting positions.

Fortunately, today more and more people are going to work because they enjoy it rather than because they need to put food on the table. Today, more than ever, we need to match what our team members actually do with what they want to do, not just what they will put up with to keep their positions.

ABOUT THIRTY YEARS AGO

I attended a seminar where the speaker (whose name I am sorry to say I have long since forgotten) made a statement that was so powerful I have remembered it word for word since that time. He said:

"I have never met a lazy person, but I have met a lot of people who appeared lazy because they weren't properly motivated."

Letting goal setters set goals and problem solvers solve problems is a major step toward motivating those who seem lazy, listless, and unmotivated. A person working in an area that he or she enjoys will be several times more *energized, happy, satisfied, fulfilled, peaceful,* and *contented* than one who has a daily fight just to keep from walking off the job in total frustration, totally ignoring the consequences.

ALLOWING THOSE AROUND YOU TO WORK THE WAY THEY WANT TO IS THE KEY TO BUILDING A TEAM

While cowriting the book *Boardroom Confidence* with Dr. Ted W. Engstrom, well-known author and President Emeritus of World Vision International, I asked him a simple question, "What is the key to building a strong team?" Dr. Engstrom has provided model leadership as the president and/or executive vice president of four major organizations and has managed hundreds of millions of dollars and thousands of people in hundreds of countries. With all that experience, he answered me in a split second, and his answer hit the very heart of the matter: "Getting round pegs in round holes."

For many fine leaders today, it is a major change in thinking to move from hiring people simply because they are available and positions need to be filled to putting the right people in the right positions based on their strengths and preferences.

Once people are in positions that fit them, you no longer have to keep motivating them. Motivation will come naturally. All you need to do is establish a few basic boundaries and give them the freedom and the resources to reach the goals or to solve the problems on which you have agreed.

Getting round pegs into round holes is a bit harder than this profoundly simple counsel seems at first. Executive assessment or people screening is *not* an easy or foolproof assignment for anyone. For some, it is downright difficult. In my twenty-plus years of consulting I have watched seasoned leaders make one simple, avoidable, extremely costly mistake possibly more than any other. What is it?

Assuming "everyone is basically like me!"

Whenever my schedule allows me to speak on a college or university campus today, I typically stop, take off my eyeglasses, pause for a short, dramatic moment, and say to the students, "I am about to tell you something that you may not think is important enough to write down, let alone memorize." Then I point to my gray hair and continue, "Do you see all of this gray hair? Today you see me as old, but you don't know how old I really am. I'm so old that I actually remember a time before McDonald's!"

Typically, the students are kind enough to chuckle a bit or at least gasp at just how old this character must really be. "What you are about to hear is extremely simple, but in my fifties I am just *beginning* to realize the depth of its meaning. These five words are so profound that I seriously doubt that I will fully understand their depth when I die."

By this time their curiosity has grown to the point

where they will at least pause to give the five words a minute's thought. Then I ask, "Would you please do this old man a favor? Please take out a piece of paper and write down these five words. Reflect on them over the years, and when you are as old as I am today, throw the piece of paper away if you want, or frame it if you like." Here are the five words:

"Everyone is not like me!"

One of the most profound but simple truths in dealing with people a person can learn, and keep learning over a lifetime, is the truth contained in that simple statement: "Everyone is not like me."

EVERYONE IS NOT LIKE ME! AND IT'S OK TO BE WHO I AM!

One of the most fundamental unspoken assumptions in the minds of most people seems to be that "everyone is fundamentally like me, or they will be when they grow up!" It is important to see differences as complementary strengths, not as immaturities.

One of the most dependable tools available to help a person see how you, I, and the next person are fundamentally different is a simple inventory known as the Role Preference Inventory.

THE ROLE PREFERENCE INVENTORY: ITS IMPLICATIONS FOR GOAL SETTERS AND PROBLEM SOLVERS

In 1973, I was working full-time on the executive team of World Vision International, a nonprofit humanitarian organization. Today, they care for hundreds of thousands of needy children around the world. My assignment, at the time, was directing the volunteer program.

While there, I designed and developed a little money container in the shape of a loaf of bread with a fish symbol embossed in the top called the Love Loaf. Your church may have participated in the program. You may have had a Love Loaf on your meal table. You may have seen one at a checkout counter at a restaurant or other place of business. World Vision now has over six thousand volunteers who service the Love Loaf in business establishments. Since its establishment, the Love Loaf program has raised tens of millions of dollars to help feed hungry people during famines, in refugee camps, and other desperate situations around the world.

In the process of developing the Love Loaf program, I concluded that over the next fifty years or so, I would likely be involved in originating and developing hundreds of such ideas. Therefore, I felt it would be wise for me to "mark my trail" by keeping track of the steps an idea goes through as it develops over time.

One day my loyal assistant, Patty Lewis, approached me in a state of rather obvious frustration. "When are you ever going to let this program settle down and become routine?" Her question actually shocked me. I had never considered such a strange idea. My immediate response was, "The day I die or the day I leave the program is probably the first day it will become routine."

I was approximately thirty-two years old at the time, and as embarrassing as it is to admit today, that was the first time it had ever dawned on me that "everyone is not like me." After that encounter it was as though I had a brand-new pair of eyeglasses to see how people differ. I discovered that I really enjoyed the design and the development phases of a program or project. But when it got into the maintenance stage, I was totally bored. However, the settled-down maintenance stage was exactly where Patty began to get comfortable with the program.

On that day, it became crystal clear to me that there are distinct phases in a project's development and that different people enjoy different phases. It is easy to predict team chemistry based on a person's preferences. Through years of observing and refining, I have identified five basic developmental phases through which each and every idea must eventually pass to reach its full potential.

DESIGN PHASE	DESIGN-DEVELOPMENT PHASE	DEVELOPMENT PHASE	DEVELOPMENT-MAINTENANCE PHASE	MAINTENANCE PHASE

Every person you know enjoys *one* phase more than the other four. The phases are mutually exclusive by definition.

1. The Design Phase

Designers prefer discussing and understanding theoretical designs. They enjoy solving theoretical problems with original theoretical solutions but don't enjoy the practical process of creating a prototype. Once a problem is solved theoretically, the burnout clock starts ticking almost immediately.

Designers tend to be problem oriented. But the problems they enjoy are theoretical problems, not the practical problems that others prefer.

2. The Design-Development Phase

Designer-developers prefer to take on a tough cause, mission, or dream and to set clear, strategic, long-range goals. They prefer to define problems, come up with original solutions, and develop a working prototype. However, near the end of the development of the prototype, they predictably hit a wall and begin to lose interest at a rapid rate. The burnout clock starts ticking loudly in a short period!

Designer-developers come as close to enjoying both goals and problems as anyone. They tend to be goal oriented but also acutely problem aware. They have close to an equal excitement about and time commitment to goals and problems.

3. The Development Phase

Developers prefer to be given clear and challenging goals and one to three working models, or examples, and adapt the best from each to create a new model that is an improvement on the existing models. But when the goal has been reached or two years and one day have passed, the burnout clock starts ticking.

Developers tend to be the most goal oriented. They rarely enjoy the process of dealing with problems.

4. The Development-Maintenance Phase

Developer-maintainers prefer to take an existing system, organization, or project and solve the practical problems, refine, debug, and improve it to the point where it is running smoothly and the results are even better than expected. But when things begin running smoothly (perhaps four or five years into a project's history), developer-maintainers want a bit more challenge.

Developer-maintainers tend to be clearly problem oriented. The problems are not the designer's theoretical problems but are down-to-earth, practical system problems. Rarely do they enjoy setting or being held accountable to reach goals.

5. The Maintenance Phase

Maintainers prefer to be given a responsibility where the policies, procedures, and systems are well defined. The burnout clock for maintainers takes twenty to thirty years to start ticking.

One other point at which maintainers burn out and want to make a change is when they are working with team members whom they perceive are not loyal, and specifically not loyal to the maintainers.

Maintainers are definitely problem oriented. But they are actually oriented to *problem prevention.* They are motivated by problems but dislike them and see them as disruptive.

Shortly after I received that insight, another revelation hit me like the proverbial ton of bricks! I was with my father, Bob Biehl, who was working as a night auditor at Shanty Creek Lodge, a world-class ski resort and golf course in Bellaire, Michigan. Since I was then living in California and didn't get to see Dad very often, I would go to work with him (all night) and chat and snack with him on his breaks.

One night he said that what he really wanted in a job was:

- to be given a specific assignment,
- to manage (lead) no one, and
- to be paid a fair wage.

That was the first time in my life it had occurred to me that, under pressure, some people don't want to be the captain of everything they are in. At the time, I fully assumed that sooner or later I would be the president of whatever I became a part of. I truly and naively assumed that everyone else really wanted the same thing. It finally dawned on me that some fully mature adults prefer to be what today I call *strong players,* others prefer to be *presidential captains,* and still others prefer to be *middle captains.*

There are three levels of leadership for each of the five developmental phases listed above:

1. *Presidential Captains:* the presidents, head coaches, and senior pastors. These leaders want to be where

the buck stops, to be the go-to person, to be fully in charge.

2. *Middle Captains:* the vice presidents, assistant coaches, and associate pastors. These people want to lead a team. Leading brings them great pleasure. They want their *own* team to lead. But under pressure, they prefer having a leader to make the final decisions.

3. *Strong Players:* those who enjoy playing the game, maybe even being the superstar. These people want their input to be respected, but they do not want to be the captain of anything, especially under pressure!

PROCESS >	Designer	Designer-Developer	Developer	Developer-Maintainer	Maintainer
LEVEL					
Presidential Captain					
Middle Captain					
Strong Player					

It is my experience that every team member prefers one of the fifteen roles shown in the grid above. When I know a person's preference, it is easy to predict that person's chemistry with the rest of the team (those who prefer one of the other roles).

The level a person prefers is not correlated to interest in goal setting or problem solving. Some people at all levels prefer goal setting, and others at all levels prefer problem solving.

I have frequently met with senior executives of an organization and asked them to *guess* the role preferences of those reporting directly to them. Then, by first names only, I begin to predict the team chemistry of the people who report to them. It is easy for me to talk for sixty minutes knowing only first names (not age, race, position, or company history) and almost never miss predicting what the natural chemistry is between people on the staff.

I have done this exercise with perhaps fifty to seventy-five senior executives. With most clients, I later have the occasion to ask each of the staff members to take the Role Preference Inventory. Some senior executives know their people so well that they guess precisely the role preferences that their team members subsequently express.

On the other hand, some senior executives are so unaware of their team members' real preferences that they miss 100 percent of their guesses. Interestingly, in many cases the executives' spouses were far more accurate than the senior executives at guessing to be the role preferences of the staff members. Those senior executives should, and wisely do, rely heavily on their spouses' instincts in selecting, understanding, and evaluating staff.

A wide variety of predictions are possible based on people's role preferences, including:

- values,
- enjoyment,
- type of creativity,
- burnout point, and
- problem or goal orientation.

These are but a few of the dimensions that are easily predicted once a person's role preference is known. Following is a grid showing a few dimensions predictable based on the phase preferred. It can help you "see behind the smile" of the person you are interviewing or who is on your staff.

As you will see by the very last row, the Role Preference Inventory can also help you predict how each of your staff members looks at goals and problems.

ROLE PREFERENCE INVENTORY

PHASE >	1. DESIGN	2. DESIGN-DEVELOPMENT	3. DEVELOPMENT	4. DEVELOPMENT-MAINTENANCE	5. MAINTENANCE
Values highly	Brilliance	Wisdom	Courage	Faithfulness	Loyalty
Likes to be thought of as	Brilliant	Wise	Courageous	Faithful	Loyal
Most enjoys this phase of a project	Designing theoretical solutions	Designing theoretical solutions, developing first the prototype	Developing a model, expanding the model	Refining the basic system, maximizing the system	Maintaining the basic model, keeping the model under control
Orientation in a new situation	Theories	Processes	Goals	Results	Control
Creativity level	Original, wants to start with a blank sheet of paper	Original, wants to start with a blank sheet of paper	Adaptive, wants to start with existing models and improve	Adaptive, wants to start with existing models and improve	Adaptive, wants to start with existing models and improve

PHASE >	1. DESIGN	2. DESIGN-DEVELOP-MENT	3. DEVELOP-MENT	4. DEVELOP-MENT-MAINTE-NANCE	5. MAINTE-NANCE
Burnout point	When a problem is solved theoretically	Seven-eighths of the way through development of the prototype	When the goal is reached or after two years on the project	Four to five years into a project or when things are going smoothly	Twenty-plus years or when the team leader or peers become disloyal
Goal or problem orientation	Problem oriented, theoretical problems	Goal oriented, problem aware, almost equal excitement about and time commitment to both	Goal oriented, little or no desire to deal with problems	Problem oriented, practical system problems, little or no desire to set goals	Problem oriented, actually problem prevention, oriented by but dislikes problems, sees as disruptive

I have discussed the correlation between role preference and goal or problem orientation with several hundred people. At the end of the discussions, I ask them if my observations about the correlation between phase of choice and preference for goal setting or problem setting make sense in their lives. I have yet to hear someone say they did not.

Find out what your staff members prefer to do and create an environment to maximize their strengths.

3

A Simple Yet Profoundly Powerful Paradigm Shift

A GOALS FOCUS VS. A PROBLEMS FOCUS: THE FUNDAMENTAL DIFFERENCE

**GOALS AND PROBLEMS
ARE
EQUALLY EFFECTIVE
IN GIVING A TEAM
A SENSE OF FOCUS!**

1. DREAM

2. RESULTS

3. FOCUS

4. GOALS	5. PROBLEMS

A brief elaboration on this basic model might be helpful:

1. Dream

Your dream is an abstract, energizing concept. It indicates a direction, but it is not measurable. It is not supposed to be measurable. In that respect, it's like a purpose that is not measurable. Purpose statements of *why* you are going to do what you're going to do and dreams, which are statements of *what* you are going to do, are like North Stars. They are intended to be guiding points in the future, but they are not intended to be measurable. A few sample dreams may be helpful:

COACH	FARMER	MEDICAL RESEARCHER	SALESPERSON	SALES MANAGER
To develop the best team that we have ever had—the perfect team	To develop the best farm possible to pass on to my children	To find a cure for cancer	To make millions of dollars and retire early	To dominate my entire district for our firm

For Christmas last year, my daughter, Kimberly, gave me a set of five CDs of cowboy music. Cowboy music is dedicated to explaining and passing on the life of the American cowboy. One song explains how a cowboy's mentor always told him, "Point the tongues of the wagons at night in the direction of the North Star." He said, "On the plains, you can lose all sense of direction during the day where everything looks the same. But if you will point your wagons toward the North Star every night, you will always know which way is north." The same is true of thinking about your dream occasionally. It keeps you going in the direction you really want to go.

2. Results

It is difficult for some people, particularly those who are more practical in their thinking, to get excited about a dream or a vision if that is their only encouragement. They are less interested in some day than in the here and now!

This is where you need to define the tangible results you are seeking. A primary result is a specific, measurable something that will exist when you are finished. Results assure you that you are making actual, practical progress toward your dream. The result you are watching and measuring needs to be clear in the minds of your team members so that they can stay on track over a period of months and years.

A few sample results might be helpful:

COACH	FARMER	MEDICAL RESEARCHER	SALESPERSON	SALES MANAGER
To win more games	To add productive acres to the farm	To conduct experiments that might lead to a cancer cure	To sell more automobiles	To sell more units

Each of the sample results could be charted on the wall of the locker room, barn, laboratory, or office. Each time a new total is added to the chart, there is a distinct feeling of positive progress toward the dream.

NOTHING MOTIVATES LIKE RESULTS!

3. Focus

Focus precedes success. Everyone agrees that a group needs a clear short-range focus that is energizing. If your dream is, generally speaking, "what difference you are going to be making some day, forty years in the future," and the result is the measurable thing(s) that will remain when you have finished, focus represents the road signs along the way. Focus is what you look at in the short range to keep you motivated toward the long range.

Again, a few specific, concrete, real-life examples:

COACH	FARMER	MEDICAL RESEARCHER	SALESPERSON	SALES MANAGER
To win more games this year, I need to *focus on increasing the average number of minutes per game that my team controls the ball.*	To add productive acres this year, I need to *focus on increasing the number of productive acres under cultivation.*	To continue conducting cancer experiments, I need to *focus on receiving grant money from major foundations.*	To sell more automobiles this year, I need to *focus on calling each of my top customers to chat about their trading plans.*	To sell more units of our product this year, I need to *focus on improving my team members' product knowledge and upgrading the product line.*

These specifically stated strategies move you in a focused way toward your primary results.

EVEN THE CHAIRMAN OF IBM KEEPS FOCUSED ON SPECIFIC STRATEGIES

Louis Gerstner, Jr., after taking over as chairman of IBM in April 1993, announced major restructuring and downsizing (IBM had lost $4.97 billion the previous year). In the course of his announcement, he said, "The last thing IBM needs right now is a vision. What IBM needs right now is a series of very tough-minded, market-driven, highly effective strategies in each of its businesses."[1]

4. Goals

One way to gain the *focus* needed in step three is to set clear, realistic, measurable goals. This is still the primary way I come to focus in my own life. For more than twenty years, I firmly believed, and taught, that it was not only one of the best ways to come to clear focus, but *the only way to come to clear focus*. I was wrong!

Remember: A *goals* focus is taking the existing program and adding to it.

COACH	FARMER	MEDICAL RESEARCHER	SALESPERSON	SALES MANAGER
To win ___ games this year, I am going to: 1. Help my team score an average of ___ points per game 2. Recruit the top ___ players available 3. Spend ___ dollars for new training equipment	To add ___ productive acres to my farm this year, I am going to: 1. Contact ___ real estate agents and have them look for available property 2. Visit at least ___ available farms 3. Buy at least ___ acres	To raise ___ dollars to fund research this year, I am going to: 1. Contact ___ foundations 2. Host ___ major fund-raising events 3. Conduct ___ experiments	To sell ___ automobiles this year, I am going to: 1. Run ___ ads in the newspaper 2. Test ___ television spots to add ___ new customers 3. Visit the factory ___ times with key customers	To sell ___ units this year, I am going to: 1. Make ___ calls per day 2. Develop at least ___ new products 3. Buy a new phone system to let me contact ___ more people per day

Each of these goals gives a person crystal-clear focus.

5. Problems

You can gain as much focus by asking, "What are the three *problems* we will solve in the next year?" as you can by asking, "What are the three *goals* we will reach in the next year?"

Remember: A *problems* approach to planning is taking the existing program and fixing problems within it.

COACH	FARMER	MEDICAL RESEARCHER	SALESPERSON	SALES MANAGER
To win ____ games this year, I am going to: 1. Help my team reduce turnovers to ____ or less per game 2. Help my team keep opponents' offenses to ____ points per game 3. Fix the broken training machines in the fitness center	To add ____ productive acres to my farm this year, I am going to: 1. Harvest ____ days earlier than last year, avoiding fall storms 2. Fix the irrigation drainage in the back forty 3. Buy an A-grade seed corn to increase my yield by 30 percent	To increase my research fund this year by ____ dollars, I am going to: 1. Re-conduct ____ experiments that were not successful last year 2. Improve my response time on thank-you letters by ____ days 3. Use my current computer to generate ____ proposals	To sell ____ automobiles this year, I am going to: 1. Call my current top ____ customers on the phone 2. Visit my top ____ current customers personally 3. Improve my sales talk by being critiqued by a local speech teacher in ____ speech lessons	To sell ____ units this year, I am going to have each salesperson: 1. Call on each existing client at least ____ times per quarter 2. Hold ____ training seminars for my sales team 3. Reduce territories by ____ percent to assure better service

It is OK to mix and match goals and problems in planning. It is also important to point out that a person, division, or organization can mix and match goals and problems in the same list of *priorities.* You can have two goals and one problem, two problems and one goal, three goals and three problems, or whatever combination is appropriate within your organizational setting.

Both goals and problems are measurable. You might ask, "Are we not just talking about a difference in terminology or a choice of words, a simple semantic difference?" Some people may use the terms interchangeably, but there is a real difference between goals and problems, as explained earlier. Goals require adding to an existing system, but problems require fixing the existing system.

THE BEST QUESTION FOR CRYSTALLIZING FUTURE PRIORITIES I HAVE BEEN ASKED IN TEN YEARS!

For the past fifteen to twenty years, I have made a hobby of collecting and, at the right time, asking profound questions.

Two or three years ago I was on a consulting day with Steve Douglass, the executive vice president for Campus Crusade, based in Orlando, Florida. Crusade has more than 40,000 staff members, a $300,000,000-plus budget, and staff in more than 150 countries.

We were just working along on some project when Steve asked me the following question:

"What *three things* can we do in the next *ninety days* to make a *50 percent* difference?"

I'll never forget coming to a screeching halt in my thoughts that day and asking Steve, "Is that a question you ask all the time?" I wondered if it was a part of the core curriculum he had studied during his undergraduate work at MIT or his MBA work at Harvard. His response was that it was not.

"Just a minute! I want to get this one down word for word," I said. Then I promised him, "I'll quote you on this one for the rest of my life."

Since that morning I have asked the question of myself or a client an average of three to five times per week for the past three years.

Ask this question a lot. Ask it of yourself. Ask it of your friends. Ask it of your team. You may want to memorize this profound question word for word. You may even want this to be the first question in your own *question collection!*

AN EXTREMELY FLEXIBLE QUESTION

You can, and should, adapt the question in many ways. For example:

What *three things* can we do in the next *ninety days* to make a . . .

- 50 percent difference by the end of this year?
- 50 percent difference by the end of the decade?
- 50 percent difference by the end of my life?

It doesn't matter one bit if you ask:

- What three *goals* can we reach in the next ninety days to make a 50 percent difference in where we are at the end of the year?
   OR
- What three *problems* can we solve in the next ninety days to make a 50 percent difference in where we are at the end of the year?

Both are great questions. Either way, you get a crystal-clear focus. But as a problem solver, you will be highly motivated by asking what three problems you can solve and just as deeply de-motivated by asking what three goals you can reach.

WHY NINETY DAYS?

You might be asking, "Why focus on ninety days?" Let me explain by first pointing out that most people:

- do not set goals at all,
- do not put in writing the problems they will solve, and
- do not have *any* written targets for the future.

Those who do tend to be people who:

- do not think in terms of decades,
- do not think in mid-range, two- to five-year priorities, and
- do not even think annually.

As you talk with people, you will find that the most common time frame for planning is the *season*. Most people ask, "What are we going to do between now and Christmas, Christmas and Easter, Easter and spring break, spring break and fall, and Thanksgiving and Christmas?" Other people think in terms of athletic seasons (football, basketball, baseball, soccer, ski, sailing, polo) or hunting seasons (duck, deer, trout). Perhaps a few people even think in terms of blueberry, mushroom, or cherry season.

That is why I put so much emphasis on the ninety-day time frame. Most people find it the easiest time frame to incorporate into their natural planning process.

GOALS AND PROBLEMS ARE NEITHER GOOD NOR BAD!

It is important for me to stop here and say that goal setting and problem solving are neither good or bad. One is not better and the other worse. One is not weaker and the other stronger. They are simply different. One may be better for you and worse for someone else, but by themselves, they are neutral.

TURKEY-FARM DEFINITION

Bigotry is automatically concluding that just because we are different (I'm a goal setter and you're a problem solver, or I'm a problem solver and you're a goal setter), you are wrong, inferior, or misguided.

Bigotry can be based on race, gender, or goal or problem orientation. In any form, it is wrong.

THE ELEPHANT STORY

It was eleven o'clock one Friday night, and I was sound asleep. The phone rang. On the other end was my friend Duane Pederson, founder of the *Hollywood Free Paper*.

"How would you like to go to Tucson tomorrow?" he asked.

"Tucson?" I groaned. "What in the world would we do in Tucson?"

"Bobby [Bobby Yerkes, a mutual friend] has a circus playing in Tucson tomorrow, and I would like to go down, get away, clear the cobwebs, and work the circus with him. We'll move some props, have a good time, and be back by ten o'clock tomorrow night."

Now there probably isn't a boy alive who hasn't dreamed about running away with the circus, so it didn't take me long to agree to go.

The next morning at seven o'clock our jet lifted off the runway at Los Angeles International Airport, headed for Tucson.

When we got there, it was a hot, dusty, windy day at the fairgrounds where the circus was playing.

We moved props from one of the three rings to the next, helped in any way we could, and generally just got dusty, dirty, tired, and hungry.

During one of the breaks, I started chatting with the man who trains animals for movies. "How is it that you can stake down a ten-ton elephant with the same size stake that you use for this little fellow?" I asked, pointing to a "small" three-hundred-pounder.

"It's easy when you know two things: Elephants actually do have great memories, but they really aren't very smart. When they are babies, we stake them down. They try to tug away from the stake maybe ten thousand times before they realize that they can't possibly get away. At that point, their elephant memory takes over and they remember for the rest of their lives that they can't get away from the stake."

We humans are sometimes like elephants. When we are young, someone says, "You're not very handsome," "You're not very pretty," or "You're not a very good leader," and ZAP!—a mental stake is driven into our minds. Often, as adults, we are still held back by some inaccurate, one-sentence stake put in our minds when we were years younger.

Today, you are an adult, so be who you are. Say what you really think. Do what you prefer doing. If you are a problem solver, be a problem solver! Say you are a problem solver and stop trying to be a goal setter. Define your future as you feel most comfortable by defining problems and solving them. You are more mature and capable than you were even twelve months ago, and next year you will be able to do things you can't do today.

If you happen to have a boss or a team leader who insists that you set goals, think through the problems you need to solve, write them out in measurable terms, and turn them in. Your boss may not easily distinguish between goals and problems. He or she may think you have completed the assignment and be very happy with your clear focus!

NOTE: The elephant running free with a stake trailing along behind is something you will never see at the circus. However, it has become the symbol of our consulting firm because it represents, in a single vivid graphic, what we are trying to do in helping you pull "elephant stakes." Let's pull some stakes together!

TEN COMMONLY HELD, DANGEROUS, COSTLY ASSUMPTIONS

Assumptions are things we *believe* to be true, whether or not they are in fact true. In the heading for this section, I called the assumptions *dangerous* and *costly*. I could also call many of them *incorrect* or *unwise*. If you accept these commonly held assumptions, they could cost you a job or a contract. They might lead you to unknowingly insult a person or damage a relationship. In fact, if you assume something that is incorrect about a person, sooner or later you will insult the person. For example, if I assume you are rich and you are really poor, or if I assume you are poor and you are really rich, sooner or later I will unintentionally insult you.

Men Are Goal Setters and Women Are Problem Solvers

It is commonly held in many families and many workplaces that men are goal setters and women are problem solvers. This assumption could not be more faulty. Many men are, in fact, goal setters, but many women are also goal setters. And many men are problem solvers, not goal setters at all.

All Problem Solving Is Serious and Complicated

If you think all problem solving is serious and complicated, read this:

OUGHTS AND ISES

A problem consists of two parts: oughts and ises. Since most problems are group problems, the most difficult part is coming to an agreement on the oughts. The problem may be written five ways:

1. The problem equals ought minus is.

A person ought *to have $14,000 to buy this car, but the fact* is *that most people have no more than $10,000—a $4,000 problem.*

2. My problem equals my ought minus my is.

I ought *to have $14,000 to buy this car, but the fact* is *that I have only $10,000—$4,000 problem.*

3. Your problem equals your ought minus your is.

You ought *to have $14,000 to buy this car, but the fact* is *that you have only $10,000—a $4,000 problem.*

4. Our problem equals our ought minus our is.

We ought *to have $14,000 to buy this car, but the fact* is *that we have a combined total of $10,000—a $4,000 problem.*

5. If ought equals is, there is no problem.

If you ought *to have $14,000 to buy this car, and the fact* is *that you have $14,000, you now own the car—no problem!*[2]

Men Are Like My Father, and
Women Are Like My Mother

Another dangerous gender assumption is that men are like my dad, and women are like my mom. Your father may be a problem solver, but the men you work with may be goal setters. Your mother may be a goal setter, but your wife may be a problem solver. The point? Each person must be evaluated as an individual and dealt with accordingly. You must not assume that because he's a man, he'll think like your father, or because she's a woman, she'll think like your mother (or like anyone else, for that matter).

One of Us Has to Be Right in Our Style,
So One of Us Has to Be Wrong

As I speak to groups (with both husbands and wives present) on the subject of Stop Setting Goals, I find couples who have been married for five, fifteen, or even thirty years who have never stopped to realize that the fundamental difference between them is that one of the mates is a goal setter and the other a problem solver. Once they realize the difference, they often elbow each other's ribs. It's as if the partners are saying to each other, "You're a goal setter and I'm a problem solver, or you're a problem solver and I'm a goal setter, and at last we've figured out why we're so different."

Sometimes those couples feel added pressure on the relationship. The reason why is they've fallen prey to the faulty assumption that one style must be right and one wrong. They might express it this way: "We're different now, but when you grow up you'll be like me because we ought to be fundamentally the same." I tell them once again, "Everyone is not like you. Your mate may be very grown-up, very mature, very adult, and simply un-like you."

Goal Setters Are the Real Leaders

I often encounter, in corporations as well as in non-profit organizations and churches, the idea that one can't be a leader without being goal oriented. It's never quite said that way, but the assumption is that the goal-oriented people are the ones who are the real leaders. That, of course, is a faulty assumption. Yes, goal setters are leaders, but so are problem solvers. Some of the fin-est leaders of our time are people who are defensive and problem oriented.

Many presidents of the United States preferred solving problems to setting goals. Many head coaches are defen-sive in their entire game strategy. Most of the CEOs of the Fortune 500 firms whom I have known personally are problem solvers, not goal setters.

Leaders Are Goal Setters and Managers Are Problem Solvers

Another incorrect assumption about leadership is that leaders are goal setters and managers are problem solv-ers. I absolutely refuse to say that there are some people who are leaders and other people who are managers. Leaders have to manage as well as lead, and managers have to lead as well as manage.

TURKEY-FARM DEFINITIONS

Leadership is knowing *what* to do next, knowing *why* it's important, and knowing *how* to bring the appropriate resources to bear on the need at hand.

Management—maximizing time, energy, and money.

On any given day, leaders spend a certain percentage of their day leading and the remainder figuring out how to maximize time, energy, and money. Every day that they work, managers spend a certain percentage of their time managing, and the rest of their time trying to figure out what to do next, why it's important, and how to bring the appropriate resources to bear on the need at hand.

All Americans Are Goal Setters

One of the discussions I've frequently had with Japanese friends and Americans who live in Japan is the distinction between the cultures of America and Japan. I've had similar conversations with the national directors of both western and eastern European nations as I've consulted in Europe on various occasions.

Nations develop stereotypes. For example, take a look at the following breakdown of a few nations that have, over decades and centuries, developed international reputations as goal-setting nations or problem-solving nations.

NATIONS (LISTED ALPHABETICALLY)	GOAL-SETTING STEREOTYPE	PROBLEM-SOLVING STEREOTYPE
Australia	X	
Canada	X	
England		X
France		X
Germany	X	
Italy		X
Japan		X
Korea		X
Switzerland	X	
United States	X	

Please do not be insulted if you are from one of these nations and you think your nation is seen differently by the majority of those looking on. These are simply my own impressions of the stereotypes of the various countries.

It is clearly possible to characterize one national culture as being goal oriented and another as being problem oriented. However, I've worked with enough goal-oriented Japanese and British leaders to know that not all Japanese leaders and not all British leaders are problem oriented, and I've worked with enough problem-solving-oriented American leaders to know that not all American leaders are goal oriented. So although we might make a generalized assumption about the kind of leadership a particular nation has, it's important to realize that there are many exceptions to that rule.

The Leader of a Country, Province, Protectorate, or Kingdom Must Be a Goal Setter

Another incorrect assumption is that to be a president, a prime minister, or a premier a person must be a goal setter. As I have studied their lives over a number of years, I have concluded that among the presidents of the United States, prime ministers of England, and premiers of Japan, perhaps as many as 50 percent were problem oriented and not goal oriented at all.

Recently, a friend told me of a book containing many of the personal letters and public speeches of Abraham Lincoln. I was fascinated by the fact that in neither of his inaugural addresses to the nation did President Lincoln mention a single goal. Rather, he delicately and gently described problems he prayed the nation could resolve during his term.

They Are Lucky to Have a Job, So They Will Do as They Are Told

A dangerous assumption within organizations is that because people need jobs, they will, therefore, do what they are told; that is, they will focus on goal setting or problem solving, or else.

The assumption is actually correct but extremely costly. It is true that most people will do what they are told if they need a job. As a problem solver, you might set goals all day long if that's what is necessary to keep paying the bills each month, regardless of how unpleasant it may be.

If your president or CEO is goal oriented and insists that all employees, including you, set goals to keep their jobs, you will no doubt set goals. However, if this is the situation, your employer is more the loser than you. The leadership is losing a tremendous amount of your natural energy and has moved you into forced, unnatural energy. The result is half the productivity for the same amount of money. So while it is true that people will set goals to keep their jobs, it is important to remember that forced goal setting is not the pathway to success.

You Must Set Goals to Be Successful

I'll never forget listening to a radio program one day when the host was interviewing someone who had made $900,000 that year and felt that he had failed. Then the host interviewed someone else who had made only $100,000 that year and felt extraordinarily successful.

As they talked, one of the things that became as clear as a flashing neon sign the size of Las Vegas was that the person who had made $900,000 and felt like a failure had set a goal of $1,000,000, and the person who had made $100,000 and felt so successful had set a goal of $90,000.

That was the day it became obvious to me that success is not absolute. It is not even measurable in the sense that some think of it—like driving a certain kind of car, living in a house of a certain value, or having a salary of a certain level. All of those things could be considered part of success if in fact you had set a goal to reach them.

When you reach goals or solve problems, you have a temporary feeling of success, but as long as you have goals or problems in the future, you have growth areas. Success this year may not be success next year because the levels change.

SUCCESS IS . . .

Success seems to be a term for which there is no commonly accepted definition. If you ask fifty people to define success, you'll probably get forty-nine different definitions.

I found this lack of a definition extremely frustrating, so one day I sat down in a coffee shop and asked myself, "What is success? What is a definition of success that would apply in a Fortune 500 company, a large church, a small church, a mom-and-pop company, a political campaign, a football team, or a volunteer organization? What is success at its essence?" Here's what I came up with:

TURKEY-FARM DEFINITION

Success is the *feeling* you get when you reach the *goals* you have set or when you solve the *problems* you decided to solve.

My definition used to be "the feeling you get when you reach the goals you have set." I've added "or solve the problems you decided to solve" for obvious reasons.

By this turkey-farm definition:

- You can know for sure if you succeeded or failed this year.
- You can evaluate big companies and start-up businesses, huge churches and small chapels.
- You define your own success level. You don't wait for others to define the "carrot" you will pursue.
- Success for you may be different from success for your parents or your siblings.

Back to the dangerous assumption. The most dangerous assumption of all is that you can't be successful without goal setting. You can. You can be very successful. You can have a feeling of success when you've solved problems that you've committed to solve.

4

Goal Setting and *Problem Solving* Are Emotional Words

I HATE SETTING GOALS, BUT I LOVE SOLVING PROBLEMS

Few words in the dictionary generate more emotion than the simple words *goals* and *problems*.

Goal setters hear the word *goals,* and they want to start toward the top of some hill. And as you know, when problem solvers hear the word *problem,* their energy level and motivation leap.

On the other hand, few words are as loaded with negative implications for the goal setter as the word *problem* or the phrase "The problem with that is . . ." Similarly, the problem solver hates the sound of the word *goal* and the statement "It's time to set our annual goals."

I HAVE HATED SETTING GOALS
ALL MY LIFE

We were in a paneled boardroom, and I was teaching the Stop Setting Goals concept to a board of directors for a powerful southeastern United States radio station.

When I got to the point in my talk where I said, "From my perspective, you never need to set another goal as long as you live," a distinguished looking and highly influential board member raised his hand. I instantaneously thought, *Uh-oh. I'm in trouble. I have just crossed some invisible line, and I'm about to be confronted at a rather emotional level.*

I nodded at him to go ahead and express his perspective.

He said, "I would like to make something clear right now, right here, once and for all." There was an emotional pause that seemed to last for days to the group (because we did not know what was about to happen) but that actually lasted only a few seconds. He finally said, with no small amount of emotion,

"I want everyone to know: I hate setting goals. I have hated setting goals all my life, and as of today, I never plan to set another."

Then he added,

"I don't mind solving problems. I actually like solving problems, but I hate setting goals."

And with that he nodded as if to say, "There, I finally got that off my chest," and sat down, obviously relieved.

So was I.

I WANT TO SCREAM WHEN
SOMEONE MENTIONS GOALS

A wife of twenty-five years relates that in the early part of her marriage, her husband encouraged personal goal-setting sessions, and she complied.

"At first, I set as many goals as he did. And I reached them all because of my perfectionistic nature. He, on the other hand, had a more balanced view of the purpose of goals and didn't knock himself out completing ones he decided were unreasonable.

"Meanwhile, I determinedly set about reaching every goal. I taught myself to play the piano, I learned French, and I completed a Ph.D. in my college major. But I was actually bored in these pursuits. I kept wondering, *Why am I pursuing these goals (laudable as they are) when it is so obvious that there is real work* around us needing to be done?

"In my mind, the *real work* was refining projects, relationships, and programs that already existed, not launching new ones.

"Now, I see I am a problem solver at heart, not a goal setter. Though all those years of pushing myself to reach goals has opened many nice vistas of personal growth and learning for me, I suspect they have taken their toll, too. As a sane, conservative, respected, forty-six-year-old woman, I surprise myself that I want to *scream* when someone mentions goals."

60 PERCENT TO 90 PERCENT OF THE PEOPLE WITHIN 100 MILES OF THE BOOK YOU ARE READING PREFER SOLVING PROBLEMS

Since I started teaching executive teams and leadership seminar groups the Stop Setting Goals concept, I have stopped in the middle of the lecture and asked those present to raise their hands indicating which they would prefer doing in the coming year if both activities were given equal respect and value: set goals and reach them or define problems and solve them.

At first, I intuitively reasoned that because they were leaders, 70 percent to 90 percent of those present would choose to set and reach goals. *Was I ever wrong!* In speaking on this topic with fifty to one hundred groups over the past three years, I have encountered *only two groups* with more than 50 percent who said they were goal setters!

As a consultant who has made his living since 1976 teaching people to set goals, as the president of an international consulting firm called Masterplanning Group, and as an author of several books on the subject, I was shocked.

With larger groups with leaders, managers, and day-to-day workers who do not care to be the team captains, the ratio is more like 80 percent to 90 percent problem solvers, 10 percent to 20 percent goal setters.

I was lecturing recently at the beautiful Michigan State University Management Center in Troy, Michigan.

It was a seminar for about a hundred community leaders on the Stop Setting Goals concept.

When I made the statement that as the president of a management consulting firm who had been teaching goal setting for more than twenty years, I believed that a person could be highly successful without ever setting another goal as long as he lived, spontaneous applause broke out in the room.

This spontaneous applause represents a tremendous pent-up frustration on the part of problem solvers who hate setting goals and experience stress, frustration, anxiety, and pressure when forced to do it. This is just one more indicator of the amount of release and relief that comes from letting goal setters set goals and problem solvers solve problems.

Mary Kay Ash is the founder of Mary Kay Cosmetics. The following was from the pen of this woman who has played a major part in changing literally millions of lives. She has changed the way a large number of Americans live and do business today. Listen to the wisdom of one of the great pioneering leaders of our generation:

Be a problem solver! Effective managers know how to recognize real problems and how to take action to solve them.
—Mary Kay Ash, *Mary Kay on People Management*[1]

PART TWO

Primary Benefits of the Stop Setting Goals Model

5

Benefits of Letting Goal Setters Set Goals and Problem Solvers Solve Problems

I was on an American Airlines 757 headed from Dallas-Fort Worth to Orange County, California's John Wayne airport, tired after a long day of consulting.

As a member of the American Airlines Platinum (frequent-flyer) Club, I sometimes receive complimentary upgrades. A few weeks earlier the Platinum desk had been kind enough to send me a few free first-class upgrade coupons, and I decided that this would be the ideal time to take advantage of the comfort of first class (at no cost to my clients) and catch a quick nap before beginning the process of documenting the day in the form of extensive notes.

Before the plane lifted off the runway, one of its road-weary passengers was sound asleep, having barely noticed the distinguished gentleman who sat down beside him.

By the time the flight attendant arrived with our

snacks, I was wide awake but needing a break before getting out my notepad and documenting the day.

I said hello to the gentleman, and as we snacked on some of American's chargrilled chicken salad and hot multigrain rolls, we began to chat.

Soon I learned that my traveling companion was in the training end of the airline business. Interested in a bit of field-testing of the Stop Setting Goals idea, I began to explain the basic insights into the subject. After telling him of my experience with Dave Ray's team that morning in Detroit and my experience with the Josh McDowell team (both described in the Introduction), I told him about the many benefits I saw in freeing problem solvers to solve problems, such as:

- maximized natural energy;
- reduced anxiety, conflict, and tension;
- increased productivity;
- increased team spirit, morale, and respect;
- improved communication;
- increased confidence; and
- increased efficiency and competitiveness.

This seasoned senior executive's comment was, "Bobb, Stop Setting Goals is a billion-dollar idea!"

Unfortunately, our paths have not crossed again since. But his comment that night was a deep encouragement in my ongoing development of the Stop Setting Goals idea.

MAXIMIZED NATURAL ENERGY

Goal setters rarely tire of working on a goal they have set personally. Of course, they may get fatigued just like everyone else, but they won't tire of pursuing a meaningful goal. While pursuing goals, goal setters are using natural energy. On the other hand, consistently working on problems requires forced energy and self-discipline for goal setters. That results in goal setters feeling drained of a great deal of natural energy.

As you know, with problem solvers, the opposite is true. When working on meaningful problems, problem solvers never seem to run out of natural energy. But when working on goals, problem solvers must rely on forced energy and tiring self-discipline. Inevitably, they will feel drained of natural energy.

One of my clients, in reviewing this manuscript, wrote the following in the margin:

> When the president comes into the office drained, I know he is dealing with problems that are keeping him from his goals. The interesting thing is that as he shares the problems, I am energized to solve them!

As a rule of thumb, it takes twice as much forced energy to accomplish a task as it does natural energy. This is why, when you are working on something you like, it seems to take hardly any energy at all. On the other hand, after working on something you do not like for the same amount of time with the same amount of progress, you feel exhausted.

Can you imagine how many dollars could be maximized in one year, worldwide, if we could figure out how to unleash natural energy and get away from exhausting forced energy?

REDUCED ANXIETY, CONFLICT, AND TENSION

Anxiety, conflict, and tension are serious sources of energy loss. When we continually try to force people who are different from us to do what we do and to like what we like, we frequently produce and experience a great deal of anxiety, conflict, and tension. Think, for example, of a problem solver trying to get goal setters to focus on the problems he or she sees.

When we accept who we are and who others are and let those who are not like us play the roles they most enjoy, we can be energized by our natural motivations and let them be energized by their natural motivations. We become a team of both goal setters and problem solvers, not a group of problem solvers resenting a group of goal setters and being resented equally in return. Everyone is better off, and the team becomes much more effective as a result.

THE RANGE WAR HAS ENDED

A few months ago the chief operating officer of a statewide association with thousands of members sat down with me at lunch. He seemed frustrated.

When I asked why, he told me, "I am a classic goal setter, but my board of directors won't talk about goals at all. They are just negative, and all they want to talk about is our problems. They are like children. We are in a constant 'range war' between my goals and their problems! I think I might start looking around for a new position."

Fortunately, some of my thoughts about goal setters and problem solvers had just become clear, and I was able to explain the distinction between goal setters and problem solvers. I explained that the board members are not negative, just defense oriented, and that he should never mention goals to this group again.

I told him, "You need to identify one main goal—what the group would agree is the ideal size for the organization ten years into the future—and then start defining the problems you need to solve to get there." His face registered instant relief. "My board is going to love this!"

I asked him to call me in a month or so to give me an update on how the board had responded. A few weeks later the phone rang, and my assistant said I had a call from my friend. His voice on the other end of the line said it all in one simple comment:

"The range war has ended!"

He went on to say that they had agreed on what they called a target for ten years in the future and had immediately focused on the problems that were roadblocks keeping them from the target. They had identified what they had to do this year, next year, and three years from now to move in the agreed-upon direction.

My friend then assigned a specific member to each problem. Today, each board member is focused, highly energized, and working hard!

INCREASED PRODUCTIVITY

Productivity has been described as painting the wall. All of the effort to get ready to paint the wall is non-productive. All of the effort to clean up after painting the wall is nonproductive. What could actually be called productive is painting the wall. The more energized, focused time a person spends painting the wall, the more productive he or she becomes.

> *When I work on problems, I come in early*
> *and leave late. When I work on goals,*
> *I come in late and leave early.*

Can you begin to imagine the number of dollars companies lose each and every day, week, month, and year, worldwide, because they so often de-motivate their teams by forcing goal setters to solve problems and problem solvers to set goals?

Get in your mind any team of which you are a part. What difference would it make in the group's productivity if for one day each of the members would:

- come to work, practice, or volunteer activity a few minutes to an hour early because they were motivated by getting to do what they most enjoy?

- remain highly motivated, rather than tense and grumpy, each of the hours they were with the group?
- stay a few minutes to an hour late because they were motivated by getting to do what they most enjoy?

Multiply that one day by a week and see how many productive hours are affected. Now multiply it by a month, a year, and ten years. Multiply that by all of the groups in your village, town, city, state, nation, and then the world!

Worldwide, we are losing billions of dollars, pounds, yen, and marks every day by forcing round pegs into square holes and square pegs into round holes.

EVEN PROBLEM-ORIENTED AEROSPACE ENGINEERS ARE MORE PRODUCTIVE WHEN SOLVING PROBLEMS!

When I was an intern for the Air Force, my engineering team was made up almost exclusively of problem solvers. When any problem arose with our multimillion-dollar space structure experiment, the whole team worked together efficiently, quickly, and effectively to solve it. Lunches were forgotten and quitting time came too soon. Solving those problems was hard work. Finding the source often required meticulous detail and everyone's brain. Fixing the problem, once found, often required everyone's muscle and dexterity. But those days are the ones I remember as really being a lot of fun.

When immediate problems were not so clearly defined,

our lunches were longer, and the clock seemed to tick more
slowly as it approached 4:00 P.M.

Ross Goebel, Aerospace Engineering Intern
Purdue University, USAF
Edwards Air Force Base, California

It is time we let problem solvers solve problems and
goal setters set goals. It is time we let defensive players
play defense and offensive players play offense. It is time
we put round pegs in round holes. We will save millions
or billions of dollars in the process and gain as much in
increased productivity.

SOME CORPORATIONS ARE PIONEERING THE WAY, FOCUSING ON PROBLEMS AS THE ROUTE TO PROFITABILITY AND IMPROVED SERVICE

Empowerment, the act of vesting substantial responsibility
in the people nearest the problems to be solved, is an exhil-
arating and awesome thing for any manager with a
healthy respect for Murphy's Law to contemplate. Nonethe-
less, the pressure for improved service quality and produc-
tivity, accentuated by the thinning of middle management
ranks, is leading an increasing number of companies to
accept it as a significant part of the answer to the question,
"How can we get more responsibility down to the front line,
where it belongs?"[1]

At Digital Equipment Corporation (DEC), there is a long
history of zeal when it comes to finding and satisfying
customer needs. It pioneered remote diagnostic services for

computer hardware and software and was the first to include twenty-four-hour-a-day telephone support as part of its customer service agreements. More than a dozen Customer Support Centers worldwide are staffed by specialists trained to diagnose and solve hardware and software problems. The system is designed to operate on one phone call and one call only. No matter which center is called or which system is involved, the first specialist to respond to a customer's request is given complete responsibility for that service call and for getting the customer's problem solved.[2]

At General Electric, it was recognized that service technicians had as many as three million contacts with customers each year, so it was important that the service work [problems] be done right the first time. As a result, the number one criterion for determining the salary of repair technicians and their managers is the grade for customer satisfaction derived from GE's follow-up contacts with service customers.[3]

At Xerox, there is a strong emphasis on product knowledge and technical training. There is also focus on problem solving. From the loading docks to the technical specialists, every Xerox employee has been through a forty-eight-hour course on problem-solving techniques as part of the company's restructuring. The training is designed to build teamwork and awareness of each employee's role in satisfying the customer.[4]

INCREASED TEAM SPIRIT, MORALE, AND RESPECT

It is also important that we stop expecting the defense to score touchdowns or the offense to hold the line. It only makes sense that we appreciate each other for our strengths and not try to force everyone to be like us.

Recently while discussing the topic of Stop Setting Goals with one of my clients, he made the following astute observation:

> Interestingly, the better the offense, the better the defense because it lets them rest (while the offense is on the field). I think I am maximized in my ability when I am around a goal setter (as long as I understand the difference). A goal setter enhances my ability to problem solve.

PROBLEMS CAN ALSO WORK TOWARD UNIFYING A TEAM

Where goals often divide a group, problem solving tends to unite a group. Whether it be in a one-on-one problem-solving effort, a group problem-solving effort, or a counseling situation. When a group is faced by a group, or individually, threatening situation . . . the group tends to bond together at an entirely deeper level.

Claude Robold, President
Mentoring Today

On each and every team where this concept has been accepted, I have observed a major increase in team spirit, morale, and mutual respect.

Rick Ensrud is the senior pastor of the rapidly growing Brooklyn Park Evangelical Free church in Brooklyn Park, Minnesota. The church has an average attendance of 750 to 1,000 people, depending on the time of year. When we first introduced the Stop Setting Goals concept to the elder board a number of years ago, there seemed to be a unanimous acceptance of the idea.

We went to the board and the staff and asked each person if they preferred setting goals or solving problems. Many were shocked, or at least very surprised, to discover who preferred setting goals and who preferred solving problems. Other members were far more obviously goal setters or problem solvers.

I explained to Rick that when someone points out a problem, the person asking the questions is not pointing an accusing finger at Rick (a goal setter) for not dealing with the problem. Instead, the person is trying to help the church grow and will not be insulted if Rick asks that person to do "draft 1" of the solution.

Since then, Rick has mentioned several times how much it helped him to know whom to ask to solve problems and whom to ask to reach goals as well as to know that his board is not being negative but is trying to help by bringing up problems.

Today, he looks forward to board meetings and sees the problem solvers on the board as allies, not troublemakers. He actually looks forward to working with them and enjoys watching them attack problems—problems that he does not want to deal with at all, problems he has been dreading.

A PLACE WHERE EVERYONE WHO HELPS SOLVE PROBLEMS GETS A SQUARE DEAL

"Most executives," says Square D Co. Chairman, President, and CEO Jerre Stead, "are well aware that tapping the power of their people is the key to succeeding against competition here and abroad."

Stead believes that can happen by involving employees in all aspects of company operations. He writes of two notable changes in particular, changes relevant to both goal setters and problem solvers:

1. *We made every employee a shareholder in the last year.*
2. *Each of our 20,000 people worldwide is invited to spend two days at our Vision College, focusing on customer service, quality, and personal responsibility.*

Why institute such changes? He writes, "Like Tom Peters, we were convinced that the era of 'if it ain't broke, don't fix it' was over. Square D had been a profitable, conservative company for 85 years. But competition was mustering strength at home and abroad. If we had waited for it to hit us broadside, it would have been too late to change."

How does he know the changes have helped? "First, by business results, such as improving productivity, assets, and space use per employee 15 percent to 20 percent each year since 1987.

"Second, by the efforts of individuals and teams. For example, an employee in South Carolina charged $2,000 to

her personal credit card to get a shipment to a nuclear power plant overnight. A production worker designed equipment that enabled one person to do a job in 14 minutes that had been taking four people 25 minutes."

Stead concludes: "During the Super Bowl last year, an employee called me at home. He wanted me to know that for 21 years he had distrusted management, but that he had just attended Vision College and it had changed everything. He now was willing to go anywhere in the company to talk about Vision/Mission and help make it happen. For me, that was the real game."

Jerre L. Stead, Chairman, President, and CEO
Square D Co.[5]

Innovative problem solving is not a new art or science. Consider what the Smith brothers did back in the 1800s.

·

PROBLEM SOLVING LEADS TO MAJOR INNOVATION—IN THE 1800S!

William and Andrew Smith had developed a popular cough drop by the late 1860s but were plagued by unscrupulous competitors who tried to capitalize on their name and product. To solve this problem, and to distinguish their product from others, the Smith brothers registered their own portraits as a trademark and had their likenesses fixed to large glass bowls that were used to display their drops at general stores and apothecary shops.

Counterfeiting continued because the jars could be filled with cheaper brand drops. Finally Andrew and William came up with a foolproof way to safeguard the integrity of

*their product in 1872, when they began selling Smith
Brothers Cough Drops in pre-packed boxes. This was the
first time that cough drops were marketed in "factory
filled" packages, and these were among the earliest confec-
tion makers of any kind to box their product. Most other
manufacturers sold their candies loose from large counter
jars.*[6]

IMPROVED COMMUNICATION

On any team where tension exists between offensive
players and defensive players, the result is major communication problems. Finger pointing and faultfinding
abound when the team loses a game, a contract, or a
member. Offensive and defensive players engage in responsibility shifting—"It wasn't our fault; it was theirs."
At the very least, a communications barrier is created.

The defensive captains need to communicate in the
language of defense (problems, quality, results, zero de-
fects, and refinement) to the defensive players. The offensive captains need to communicate in the language of
offense (goals, records, scoring, success, and sales) to
the offensive players. The offensive and defensive captains need to work together as a team rather than being
upset because everyone isn't playing offense, or everyone isn't playing defense.

INCREASED COMMUNICATION AND TRAINING SAVED MOTOROLA THREE BILLION DOLLARS!

The multibillion-dollar electronics corporation Motorola conducts training programs from Motorola University, a collection of computer-equipped classrooms and laboratories at the corporate headquarters in Schaumburg, Illinois, and regional campuses in Arizona and Texas. Motorola U. trains employees, suppliers, and customers.

Motorola calculates that every one dollar it spends on training delivers thirty dollars in productivity gains within three years. Since 1987 the company has cut costs by more than three billion dollars largely by training employees to simplify processes and reduce waste.

Most courses at Motorola U. are highly technical but also include training in "soft skills" such as communication and cooperation. Says Edward Bales, Motorola's chief liaison to schools and universities, "We teach collaborative problem solving. In school that's called cheating."[7]

INCREASED CONFIDENCE

Whenever we are playing or working in our strength area (goal setters working on goals, problem solvers solving problems), we feel strong. Offensive players playing defense and defensive players playing offense feel weak. We have double the confidence in our strength area.

When your team gets to the point in its development where individual members can rely on the strengths of their teammates, the group will be far more confident as a team. If players with offensive instincts are playing offense and players with defensive instincts are playing defense, your team strength is maximized. You can count on your teammates to be at their greatest strengths, and you are in a position to contribute your best. True team confidence begins there.

INCREASED EFFICIENCY AND COMPETITIVENESS

Focusing on problem solving and refining is the key to any firm's or country's competitiveness in the world market.

PROCESS AND CONTINUOUS PROBLEM SOLVING ARE THE KEYS TO INCREASED EFFICIENCY AND COMPETITIVENESS

The secret of America's future competitiveness does not lie in dazzling scientific and technological breakthroughs but instead will be the result of step-by-step work that improves existing products and the way they are manufactured.

Mastering this "cyclic development process" is critical to our country's ability to compete, according to Ralph Gomory, president of the Sloan Foundation and former IBM senior VP for science and technology. Gomory recently spoke at a two-day Stanford University conference on "Economic Growth and the Commercialization of New

Technologies," sponsored by the Technology and Economic Growth Program of Stanford's Center for Economic Policy Research.

Scientific innovations have produced great new technologies, such as the invention of the transistor or the semiconductor. But our fascination with big breakthroughs also has produced a "mythology" about the enduring economic impact of these inventions, Gomory observed. "We are okay at getting things started—but not at winning the longer race."

The innovation process is dominated by the scientists building a product around a new idea. The cyclical process is dominated by the manufacturing engineers making incremental improvements to existing products. "It is in this area where we have significant problems today," Gomory said.[8]

PART THREE

Team Implications of the Stop Setting Goals Model

6

A Great Team Needs a Strong Offense and a Strong Defense

Goal setters instinctively think offense.

Problem solvers instinctively think defense.

And they have since the *fourth-grade playground!*

What were you like in the fourth grade? Have you ever wondered how your fourth-grade experience shaped your adult leadership style and adult comfort zones? (Comfort zones are simply areas and activities in which you feel most comfortable.)

A couple of years ago, I wrote a book for Thomas Nelson Publishers called *Why You Do What You Do*. In the process of doing research for the book, I interviewed several hundred healthy, balanced executive-level leaders, asking them many questions as I tried to establish the basic motivations behind their adult behavior.

One of the shocking insights that came out of those hundreds of hours of behind-the-defenses conversations, guided by a loosely structured questionnaire, was

the amazingly high percentage of adult leadership patterns that traced back to around the third, *fourth,* and
fifth grades.

Why the third, fourth, and fifth grades? I firmly believe that personal confidence, or the lack of it, is the
result of our preschool years. Our ability to adjust to
institutions outside the home develops in kindergarten
through the second grade. ("What's recess?" "Where is
the bathroom?" "Should I bring a blanket to school?")

However, our social skills and our ability to provide
natural and comfortable leadership developed on the
playground at recess or after school in the third, fourth,
and fifth grades. Think about the difference in physical
skills and team playing skills required for T-ball and
baseball.

We learn in the fourth grade whether or not people
will follow us and whether we like to score points or
keep others from scoring. We learn whether we feel
most comfortable playing with boys or girls and even
whether we are more comfortable relating to adults than
to other children.

We were offensive or defensive in our instincts, our
preferences, or play patterns by the fourth grade, and
that orientation rarely changes as we mature into adult
leadership roles.

It is also possible to begin to identify the preferences
of our children and our grandchildren by the fourth
grade and to begin to help them work with their natural
preferences, not against them.

The questions below will help you get a quick feel for
how fourth-grade playground patterns parallel, and predict, adult leadership patterns.

THE FOURTH-GRADE PLAYGROUND PROVIDES CLEAR AND RELIABLE INDICATORS OF ADULT LEADERSHIP STYLES AND COMFORT ZONES

What were your fourth-grade comfort zones? (Stop and think about it for a few minutes.)

- What were you really like in the fourth grade?
- What did you do most?
- What did you enjoy most?
- Whom did you enjoy most?
- Did you feel most comfortable with adults or other children?
- What subculture were you most comfortable in as a child?

Can you see parallels between your fourth-grade comfort zones and your adult comfort zones?

1. What *role* did you play on the playground at recess or after school when the adult teachers were not around to supervise your play activities? Were you:

   ☐ the captain of everything—the organizer?
   ☐ on the team but not the captain—supportive, a solid player?
   ☐ off to the side, not playing the game, but watching—a cheerleader?
   ☐ playing house with just a few friends?
   ☐ a loner who didn't care what the other children were doing?
   ☐ other _____

Question: can you see a parallel between the fourth-grade role you were most comfortable playing and your comfort zones today as an adult?

2. What were your most comfortable *social-relation-ship patterns?* Were you a child who:

    ☐ always had one best friend?
    ☐ always had three friends with whom you seemed inseparable?
    ☐ was always friendly to everyone but close to no one?
    ☐ always alone?
    ☐ always stayed with family members?
    ☐ other _____

Question: Can you see a direct parallel between the relational comfort zone you had in the fourth grade and your social preferences today?

3. Did you spend most of your time with boys or with girls? Or did you spend roughly the same amount of time with both?

    ☐ most of time with boys
    ☐ most of time with girls
    ☐ about 50/50
    ☐ other _____

If you related most of the time to boys (doing "rat killin' and other boy things," as a friend and client from Lubbock, Texas, calls it in his west Texas way), you are most comfortable with men as an adult. If you related mostly to girls, you are most comfortable with women today. If you related to both about the same, you are equally comfortable with men and women as an adult.

That is why many women who grew up mainly with brothers and their brothers' male friends may be far more comfortable being with, and relating to, men than with other women.

It is also why many men who grew up mainly with sisters and their sisters' female friends may be far more comfortable relating to women than to other men.

4. Did the teams you played on typically *win, lose,* or *draw?*

☐ We always seemed to win!
☐ We always seemed to lose!
☐ We just had fun—sometimes we won, and sometimes we lost!
☐ Other _____

You will actually feel most comfortable with a team today that parallels your fourth-grade team. That is one reason why some players choke in the championships.

5. Did you grow up in a *subculture?* Was your subculture:

☐ ethnic?
☐ farm community?
☐ inner city?
☐ nationalistic?
☐ regional?

☐ religious?
☐ other _____

You may relate very comfortably to other subcultures today, but do you still feel most comfortable in the subculture of your childhood? Under pressure, you may yearn to return to and be a part of your childhood subculture.

6. Did you relate better to:

☐ adults?
☐ peers?
☐ kids older than you?
☐ kids your age?
☐ kids younger than you?
☐ other _____

If you related better to adults as a child, as an adult you are probably more comfortable with (and care more about the opinions of) authority figures and older people. If you related better to other children in the fourth grade, as an adult you are probably more comfortable with (and care more about the opinions of) your peers than authority figures.

7. Did things *revolve around you as a child* (because you were an only child, a strong child on the playground, a super athlete, etc.), or *did you revolve around someone else's agenda?*

☐ I was the very center of my universe. Things revolved around me and my agenda.

☐ I responded to someone else's agenda most of the time.
☐ Both were true in my family situation.
☐ Other _____

Egocentric adults, those who assume the agenda will revolve around them, were typically children around whom things were already revolving by the fourth grade.

8. Did you grow up feeling *rich, poor,* or *in between?* As a child I clearly remember feeling that our family was:

☐ rich.
☐ well off but certainly not rich.
☐ average financially.
☐ working class.
☐ not hungry but poor.
☐ hungry and poor.
☐ other _____

If you grew up feeling rich and as an adult you feel poor, you will tend to feel out of place. If you grew up poor and have a lot of money as an adult, you will likely feel just as out of place.

9. With your siblings and friends, did you *always lead* or *never lead?*

☐ always led
☐ never led
☐ about 50/50
☐ other _____

If you always led your siblings and friends in childhood, you will feel most comfortable leading them as adults today. If you never led them, you may feel uncomfortable leading them today—even if your profession calls on you to lead a much higher percentage of the time than they do at this point.

10. Did you instinctively want to *score points* or to *keep someone else from scoring?*

    ☐ My instinct was to score points.
    ☐ My instinct was to keep others from scoring.
    ☐ I enjoyed offense and defense about the same.
    ☐ I wanted just to enjoy the game, whether I scored or kept others from scoring.
    ☐ Other _____

If you wanted to score points as a fourth grader, chances are very high that you are a *goal setter* today. If you wanted to keep others from scoring as a fourth grader, chances are very high that you are a *problem solver* today.

NOTE: Just because an activity is not in your comfort zone does not mean you aren't able to do it. It just means that it is less comfortable for you. When you get tired or are under pressure, you will more than likely want to return to the comfort zones of your fourth grade.

Incidentally, the reason the parallels between your fourth-grade patterns and your adult comfort zones are so important is that they can help you see just how deeply ingrained your preference for goal setting or problem solving is. If one or the other has been your preference since the fourth grade, chances are it will not change anytime soon.

The situation is the same with each member of your team. Your goal setters will remain goal setters. Your problem solvers will remain problem solvers. You can pressure, intimidate, threaten, embarrass, pray, or do anything else you like, but you are not likely to change members of your team from their childhood preference.

If you do get a few people to change on a temporary basis, when the pressure is on, they will revert to their childhood comfort zones. Goal setters will set goals. Problem solvers will abandon the goals and focus on the problems at hand.

REMEMBERING THE FOURTH GRADE RESTORES CONFIDENCE TO ADULT YEARS

A wonderful mother of three was concerned about how her fourth-grade patterns affected her as an adult. After discussing the fourth-grade parallels for a while, she explained that her junior-high and senior-high years had been extremely difficult.

Junior-high and senior-high years could be called "the years of the masks." Those years rarely affect adult leadership patterns in a major way. In some ways, the teen years are exceptions, fantasies, and flukes. "If you will go back to your childhood," I told the woman, "and see what your life was like in the fourth grade, you will see the real level of leadership and confidence that you are most comfortable with."

She followed my advice, and she felt tremendous surprise as she recalled her leadership roles and healthy relationships in elementary school. The trauma of her turbulent teen years in junior high and senior high had all but erased those good fourth-grade memories. But when she studied the memories carefully, her childhood confidence actually began to return. She felt release from the bogeyman of her distressing teen years.

If you cannot remember your fourth grade, no matter how hard you try, go ahead and use the fifth grade (or the earliest grade you can remember). Most people find it difficult to remember kindergarten and the first, second, and third grades. They remember more clearly the fourth, fifth, and sixth grades.

Ask yourself the following questions to help you focus on the fourth grade:

- Where did I live?
- Who was my teacher?
- Who were my best friends?
- What did we play?
- Where did we play?

The questions can help you begin to recall what your fourth-grade experience was really like. It may also be helpful on occasion to talk with your parents or your siblings, particularly older siblings, to get a view of how you related to others when you were in the fourth grade. Ask:

- What did you see me do?
- What didn't you see that you thought you should have?
- How did I play with other kids?

Family members often recall stories that can help restore your memory and your understanding of what you were like in the fourth grade. As you get in touch with your fourth-grade experience, you will begin to see a lot of parallels between your comfort zones then and your comfort zones as an adult.

As a leader, if you want to begin to understand and assess the natural leadership styles and comfort zones of your team members, ask each of them the ten questions beginning on page 87. Discuss the questions with your team to give each member a deeper understanding of the other members and how you can work together as a team.

Great coaches work with natural instincts. Both professional and college coaches often take a player who has played offense at a lower level and shift him or her to defense, or vice versa, to determine whether the player's instincts are clearly offensive or defensive.

REMEMBER: A great team needs a strong offense (goal setters) and a strong defense (problem solvers) to win a championship.

IT WOULD BE LIKE LETTING A BIRD OUT OF A CAGE!

One of the frequent experiences that people have in our seminars is realizing for the first time that they were goal oriented as children but have been working professionally in an area that is problem oriented. Just the thought of being in a goal-oriented position is exciting to them.

The other day a man said to me, "I solve problems every day because I'm good at it. But as a child I was a very aggressive offensive player. I was the quarterback and always focused on scoring points." He asked, "How does my childhood square with my adult role?"

I asked, "How would you feel today if you were reassigned at work and your new role required you to set your own goals and to set the goals for your team? How would that make you feel? Would you feel drained or excited?"

His response surprised his friends, who saw him as a world-class problem solver who loved problem solving. He paused for a reflective moment and then told the group with genuine excitement in his voice:

"It would be like letting a bird out of a cage!"

A SPECIAL NOTE ABOUT THE FOURTH GRADE TO PARENTS

Whenever I talk about the implications of the fourth-grade experience for adult behavior patterns, inevitably someone comes up after the lecture and asks, "What are the implications for my children today? What can I do to help them the most without 'programming them'?" Perhaps you've been wondering the same thing.

Let me tell you what I tell them. First of all, love your children without conditions. They need to learn that there are consequences to their behavior. But try never to let them feel that rejection or withheld love is a potential consequence. Do not give them the impression that your love is conditional, based on their performance.

Second, help them become really, really good at doing something that fits their strengths and body style. Children don't have the objectivity to identify their strengths and predict the implications for future activity. They typically do not know if they could actually become a pro football player, chess champion, chemist, or business leader. They do not understand the implications of hereditary height, body style, hand size, and so forth. They need your help to plug into an activity that fits them.

Third, expose your elementary school children to a healthy variety of situations: where they play with older and younger children, boys and girls; where they lead or where they follow; where they have enough money and where they learn that "money does not grow on trees"; just to name few.

Fourth, give your children positive pet names, nick-names, or special names that only you call only them only when you are alone together. If they should ever be in real trouble emotionally as teenagers, calling them by their pet names when you are alone with them breaks through teenage masks like a smooth key in a well-oiled lock.

A few words to grandparents, godparents, aunts, un-cles, and neighbors: If you care for children, keep in mind the four pointers I've described. No matter how hard their home life may be, children will come through in much better shape if there is an adult somewhere who gives them a pet name, loves them, and thinks they are special.

I have talked with literally hundreds, approaching thousands, of people about their childhood experiences. Many had dysfunctional, traumatic childhoods. But they often had one schoolteacher, Sunday school teacher, aunt, uncle, or friend who really cared, and that made all the difference in the world!

You make a significant difference with children who know that you love them and will care if they live or die for as long as you live.

Now, back to goal setting and problem solving!

FREQUENTLY, GOAL SETTERS LOOK DOWN ON PROBLEM SOLVERS AND PROBLEM SOLVERS LOOK DOWN ON GOAL SETTERS, DIVIDING THE TEAM AGAINST ITSELF!

Have you ever felt others looking down on you because you were not like them? You sensed that because of the difference, they automatically concluded that you were not quite as good as they. Have you been a part of a team divided between those who were aggressive goal setters and those who were aggressive problem solvers? If you are old enough to read a book like this, the answers to those questions are likely *yes!*

How many times have you seen athletes interviewed on television after a game and heard offensive players blame the defense for the loss or defensive players blame the offense? It is easy to blame people on the team who are different from us—easier than to recognize our own inability to cooperate with those who are different.

At a recent lecture on Stop Setting Goals in Minneapolis, a woman who appeared rather shy raised her hand and asked permission to ask a question. I gave her a nod, and she asked the question on behalf of many others who didn't want to ask but obviously agreed with her unspoken assumption: "Bobb, do you think goal setters look down on problem solvers?"

For dramatic effect, I allowed the room to get as quiet as midnight in Mancelona. I paused as though searching for an answer and then said with no uncertainty, "Absolutely!"

I asked her if she would mind answering a question

for me in return. A little surprised and, I think, slightly uneasy, she paused and then nodded her consent. I asked her, "At the same time, do you think problem solvers look down on goal setters?"

She rolled her eyes toward the ceiling, and then after a brief reflective pause, she replied, "Absolutely!"

That brief public conversation contained an unfortunate insight into the way goal setters and problem solvers all too frequently look at one another.

Goal setters need problem solvers, and problem solvers need goal setters to turn common dreams into reality.

The fact is that goal setters need problem solvers to solve problems so that they aren't stuck solving all of those problems themselves. At the same time, problem solvers need goal setters, or else the problem solvers had better set some goals.

The defense needs the offense, and the offense needs the defense. Wise coaches and quarterbacks thank both the offensive unit and the defensive unit when in the media limelight.

PRETTY PLEASE!

Recently, I had lunch with a successful, distinguished looking gentleman in his mid-fifties who looked physically fit enough to suit up and play some big-time football. Today, he is the CEO of a successful retail chain, a real estate owner, and a restaurateur, just to name a few of his ventures.

During lunch he recounted this wonderful story from his days in college football.

"I had the privilege of being a blocking back for one of the finest fullbacks ever to play the game. In his junior year he was an all-American. I really enjoyed being a starter on the team and look back with great satisfaction on our winning seasons."

He continued, "However, there came a point in our best season when the all-American began to get the big head. One day our team had had all of his ego trip we could take, so we devised a plan. No one would block for Mr. Bigshot!

"He came back to the huddle, a few plays into the first quarter, with a very frightened and very humble look in his eyes. 'What's wrong?' he asked, knowing full well what was happening. A few plays later he returned to the huddle, looking a bit more frightened and a lot more humble. 'What do you want from me?' he pleaded.

"It was my job to be the team's spokesman, so I explained, 'We want you to say pretty please!' He asked (well, he actually begged!), 'Pretty please, would you start blocking for me?'

"We started blocking. We won the conference championship. He went on to play professional football, a little bit humbler. I remember this story each and every time I am tempted to feel I could run any one of my many companies by myself."

Goal setters frequently ask, verbally or mentally:

"Why are problem solvers always so negative?"

As you know by now, problem solvers are not negative, they just look at the defensive side of the field.

Most goals setters do not realize that when problem solvers bring up a problem, many times they are secretly hoping the problem they bring up will be assigned to them. They are not accusing the goal setter of ignoring the problem.

Problem solvers are not negative people. They are focused on keeping problems scoreless against the team.

On the other hand, problem solvers often ask, verbally or mentally:

"Why are we setting goals again? You didn't follow through last time."

Goal setters may not make each and every goal, but without goals we would never add fresh new dimensions to our organizations.

When goal setters and problem solvers can see one another as teammates and not as enemies, then, and only then, a team can come together! Goal setters are like the gas. Problem solvers are like the brake. You need both. If you have all gas, you will go 160 miles per hour and drive off a cliff. If you have all brakes, you will never get off the dime. You need both, and you need to know when to use each.

PROBLEM SOLVERS WANT TO WIN JUST AS MUCH AS GOAL SETTERS

Any linebacker who has ever played in the National Football League wanted to win the Super Bowl championship ring as much as the offensive players on his team. But the linebacker's thinking since the fourth grade has been, more than likely, keeping someone else from scoring points.

Players, coaches, teams, and leaders in all fields must understand how to capture and channel the tremendous energy of their problem solvers, or their teams will never be as good as they could and should be.

DO NOT CONFUSE DEFENSIVE WITH PASSIVE

Problem solvers are just as *aggressive* as goal setters! The defensive captain on a football team is typically just as aggressive as the offensive captain.

ONE AGGRESSIVE PROBLEM SOLVER

Marsh Fisher, inventor of the problem-solving software program called Idea-Fisher, was born on a farm back in 1925. He lived and worked according to the soil and the seasons before leaving to become an entrepreneurial legend. . . .

After beginning work on Idea-Fisher, its creator took time out to become rich. His work as a real estate salesman gave him the idea for Century 21, which he helped to found in 1972.

He retired to Honolulu, with several million dollars, expecting "to lie on the beach and suck coconuts and play golf." But his idea obsessed him, so he placed advertisements in the Honolulu Advertiser for creative people to help him brainstorm. Soon he had three shifts of people per day coming into his house. . . . What he was aiming to create was "a system, a natural system, based on the way the mind really stores things."

In all, it took him twelve years and $4 million to create the program. Fortunately, the kind of computer technology that could handle the program was developing, unbeknownst to Fisher.

Today, Fisher notes that management training is beginning to place heavy emphasis on creativity and problem solving. Moreover, he says, the Japanese are getting to the point in their technological development where they are about to "stop imitating and start inventing."

"We now have no choice. . . . You've got to get comfortable with problem solving and have the tools and systems that make you look forward to problems."[1]

7

Goal Setters and Problem Solvers Need Dreams, Confidence, and Success

WHAT IS YOUR TEAM'S CLEAR ENERGIZING DREAM?

Do you remember the dreams from Chapter 3?

COACH	FARMER	MEDICAL RESEARCHER	SALESPERSON	SALES MANAGER
To develop the best team that we have ever had—the perfect team	To develop the best farm possible to pass on to my children	To find a cure for cancer	To make millions of dollars and retire early	To dominate my entire district for our firm

A fundamental need for all teams is to have a dream that is bigger than any one of the team members, no matter how much of a superstar one or more team members appear to be.

Many teams (work teams, sports teams, volunteer teams, and church teams) do not have a crystal-clear dream. If you are a team leader, develop a dream that is big enough to get goal setters and problem solvers to see that they need one another and to experience the real in-the-trenches need to work closely together. A team needs to have a dream that is so big that the offense and the defense desperately need each other to win.

Dream no small dreams for they have no power to move the hearts of men.
—Johann Wolfgang Von Goethe

Defining your team's dream may take a considerable amount of time, but as a leader it is critical for you to define a dream for your team. Probably the most frequent reaction I get when discussing the development of a dream is, "I know I need a dream, but how in the world do you go about defining your dream?"

You might find the following question helpful to you in the process of clarifying your personal dream or your team's dream:

The dream-defining question: How can we make the most significant difference during our time on this team?

Your team's dream, clearly understood, will energize the team. Your dream can be as energizing to your team as the thought of winning a national championship is to a professional sports team.

A dream is what generates the excitement of baseball's World Series, football's Super Bowl, hockey's Stanley Cup, soccer's World Cup, the auto industry's Car of the Year award, the motion picture industry's Oscar, and the music industry's Grammy.

Without an energizing dream of accomplishing some important feat, some major milestone, some top-of-the-hill experience that cannot be accomplished alone, a team tends to develop petty differences and eventually divides against itself. One of the most frequent divisions, of course, is of the goal setters against the problem solvers, the risk takers against the faithful, task-oriented workers. It is essential, with any team you are leading, to overcome these differences by defining a dream that is worthy of the whole team.

A DREAM PROVIDES ENERGY FOR A TEAM

If the members of a team have a dream of winning a national championship, they have nearly endless energy for early morning practice, late night practice, sit-ups, push-ups, quizzes, reviews, briefs, and all kinds of things. But if there is no dream, the team is without energy, lifeless, listless, and plodding along.

A DREAM HELPS YOUR TEAM MOVE
BEYOND PETTY DIFFERENCES

I'll never forget playing football in high school. We would have all kinds of differences on the team during the week—jockeying for positions, joking back and forth, and, if a couple of teammates were especially testy, even an occasional inner-squad fistfight.

But we moved beyond that when we moved beyond our scrubby old practice uniforms. We climbed into the crisp, clean, bright Mancelona Ironmen orange-and-black uniforms and snapped on the chin straps of the shiny orange-and-black Ironmen helmets every Friday night to defend the honor of Mancelona High School. Our differences melted into a common resolve. We were committed, as a team, to do battle against other mighty little villages such as Harbor Springs, Charlevoix, Boyne City, and Pellston.

Every Friday night, everyone became a part of the dream, a part of the team. The band gave us emotional music. The fans gave us wild cheering. The offense gave points. The defense gave sacks. The coaches gave direction. We were one team every Friday night in Michigan's version of Garrison Keillor's Lake Wobegone.

We knew that every kid playing offense desperately needed every kid playing defense in order to win, and we dreamed of having a winning season. The dream of a winning season made those frigid northern Michigan fall practices bearable.

TEAM AND PERSONAL CONFIDENCE IS A BY-PRODUCT OF PREDICTABILITY

One means to predictability is a plan based on goals to be reached. Another is a plan based on problems to be solved.

Have you ever struggled with wavering confidence? If you are human, the answer is probably yes. Every individual and team needs a sense of confidence to function properly. But where does confidence come from? What conditions are present when you feel confident? What conditions are present when you don't?

Confidence is a by-product of predictability. A plan (involving goals or problems) increases confidence.

When I first tell people that confidence is a by-product of predictability, the most typical response I get is a blank stare. The question in their eyes is, "Huh?"

The best way I know to explain the principle is with a few what-ifs.

What if:

- you were a marathon runner,
- you have won every race you have run for the past three years, and
- you feel 100 percent healthy?

Your knees are predictable, so you run with confidence!
What if:

- during a marathon your knee pops out at mile marker eighteen,
- you go sprawling into the cinders, and
- your knee is in a brace for the next three months?

Your knee is not predictable, so you run with less confidence.
What if:

- you train hard, and
- a year later you are winning again?

Your running confidence returns to 99 percent of your confidence level before the accident.
What if:

- during your first marathon after the accident you are feeling great,
- on mile marker ten your knee goes again, and
- you fall into the cinders?

You will never again run with the same degree of confidence. You have knees with limited predictability; therefore, you have limited running confidence.

Confidence is a by-product of predictability!

There are several ways to develop predictability in life. Here are a few examples:

SITUATION	PREDICTABILITY	CONFIDENCE
Money in the bank	Predictable that I can pay my bills on time	Financial confidence is high
Physically strong	Predictable that I can finish the race	Physical confidence is high
Spouse loves me	Predictable that my spouse will accept me when I get home	Marital confidence is high
I have lots of friends that I have known for years	Predictable that my friends will not reject me, even if I don't say exactly the right thing at the party	Social confidence is high
I have a crystal-clear plan for the future	Predictable that I know exactly what I am supposed to do to get where I want to arrive	Life confidence is high

In the past, a few common assumptions I made were:

- I need goals to develop a plan.
- I need a plan to feel confident.
- Therefore, I need goals to feel confident.

However, it is now obvious to me that:

- One way to increase predictability is to have a plan.
- One way to develop a plan is to write out my goals.
- One fresh alternative way to develop a plan is to write out the problems I will solve in the future.

- Either way, the future is clear and predictable, so my confidence is stronger.

A plan made up of problems is less risky than one made up of new goals and is even more energizing for problem solvers. Goal setters typically require a little risk to make things interesting, but problem solvers are energized by the problem itself, not the risk of something new and untried.

In what area is your confidence faltering right now? Do *not* try to "pump up your confidence." Look at new ways to increase predictability in that area, and your confidence will return automatically. If it is a new area, develop predictability and watch your confidence grow!

BUILDING AN ORGANIZATION ON PROBLEMS

As a problem solver, have you ever asked yourself, "If I'm not a goal setter, how can I ever expect to be president of a company?" If you're a problem solver who wants to be president, this chapter has some good news for you.

It is just as realistic to build an organization focusing on problems (quality and service) as it is to build one focusing on goals (expansive growth), once you reach the "pull phase."

A PRESIDENT CAN BE A GOAL SETTER
OR A PROBLEM SOLVER

Jack Welch, CEO of General Electric, says, "Companies in the '90s will have global reach and global distribution—and will have a workforce and organization centered around productivity goals . . . productivity improvement is infinite. It is a product of ideas. At GE, our productivity is increasing; our speed is increasing; and our involvement with our employees is increasing."

GE uses a 360-degree Leadership Assessment form for its employees. One of the characteristics of a leader is initiative, and one of the listed performance criteria is "anticipates problems and initiates new and better ways of doing things."[1]

THE PUSH/PULL MODEL

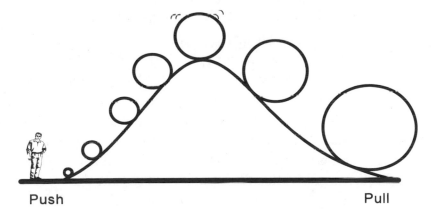

Push   Pull

A word of explanation about the Push/Pull Model above might be helpful right here. Imagine for a minute a man at the bottom of a long, smooth hill. The hill slopes gradually, but the farther you go up the hill, the steeper it becomes. The hill is covered with snow that is perfect for packing into snowballs and for making snowmen with corncob pipes in their mouths. The man starts rolling a snowball up the hill (starts a business, club, church, other organization). The farther he goes up the hill, the larger the snowball becomes. Eventually the snowball is *huge,* maybe twenty feet high. This is the *push phase.*

Just before the man reaches the peak of the hill, he gets the feeling that if he doesn't push every single second, the snowball will begin to roll back down the hill, taking him with it. In the push phase, you have to push each and every day, or everything you are doing will go backward: the business will go away, and people will stop calling or coming. This phase often requires goal setting for focusing the future and providing motivation.

When the man comes to the top of the hill, the snowball teeters on the peak. The man cannot predict whether the snowball will roll back down the hill or start rolling with increasing speed down the other side.

Then, slowly at first, the huge ball of snow starts rolling down the other side of the hill. The farther it goes, the faster it rolls. The man starts running to keep up with it. The farther it goes, the bigger it gets. The bigger it gets, the faster it rolls. This is the *pull phase.* There are problems to solve during the push phase, but there are a lot more to solve during the pull phase.

Once your organization reaches the pull phase, where you are running to keep up, you can easily switch to a *problem solving focus,* and the organization will keep growing if there is a strong demand for your product or service. If a team simply solves the problems in a strong organization, the organization will grow and create more growth problems without going through a formal goal-setting exercise. For a predominantly problem-oriented team, this approach might be much more energizing and motivational than having clearly stated goals.

A CEO WHO BUILT AN ORGANIZATION FROM THE GROUND UP AND HAS RESISTED SETTING GOALS EVERY STEP OF THE WAY

I recently had lunch at a local country club with a highly visible friend of many years. He is the CEO and chairman of the board of a one-hundred-million-dollar-a-year organization, and he built the organization from the ground up while resisting setting goals every step of the way!

The topic of conversation drifted to the Stop Setting Goals idea. Once I had drawn the diagram on page 113 on his legal pad and my friend understood the fundamental differences involved, he immediately said: "I guess you know which I am. I am clearly a problem solver. Have you ever known me to set a goal as long as you've known me? Do you see now why I've resisted your suggestions that we set goals? My main concern has always been quality. I wanted a consistent two-day turnaround on all our mail, phone orders—everything to do with serving the people we have as constituents, and I haven't cared to build a big empire.

"The fact that we are a one hundred-million-dollar-a-year enterprise has nothing to do with goal setting.

"It has everything to do with the fact that we started small and kept solving problems. The bigger the organization became, the bigger the problems became, and the harder we worked to move toward a two-day turn-around on all orders, whether we had two orders or fifty thousand phone calls in one day.

"I have been, am, and will be a problem solver, not a goal setter."

That conversation illustrates the fact that even the founders and presidents of organizations can build huge organizations and never think in terms of goal setting at all. Many top leaders of our time—including presidents of organizations, senior pastors, presidents of countries, representatives, senators, mayors, and coaches—are defense and problem oriented in their thinking.

You can build an organization with revenues in the billions by focusing on solving problems. As a matter of fact, of all the Fortune 500 company presidents that I have met, the majority are problem oriented, and not goal oriented at all. Their focus is "How do we solve the problems we've got?" not "How do we reach new goals?" Are all Fortune 500 company presidents and CEOs problem oriented? Of course not. But are many of them? Absolutely, including some company founders.

Once your organization reaches a critical size, assuming there is a need for your product or service, it can grow as fast by focusing on problems as it can by focusing on goals.

SUCCESS IS 10 PERCENT ABILITY, 30 PERCENT CREDIBILITY, AND 60 PERCENT VISIBILITY

Warning: If your visibility exceeds your ability, it will destroy your credibility!

In Santa Monica, California, not far from the ocean, a small restaurant was prepared for business. Its owners and staff hurriedly prepared the environment, the menu, and all the things necessary to make this restaurant *the* most talked about avant-garde restaurant in all of southern California. Opening night came, and the staff had, in fact, developed the *ability* to serve food. They had the equipment, the tables, the napkins, the help, the chefs— everything to make opening night an unforgettable event. They had the ability.

What's more, every person that came was delighted with the food, the service, the ambiance—everything. They started telling their friends. A few weeks later, the restaurant had a healthy, thriving, growing business, and everyone who came said the same thing: "It's awesome. It's wonderful! We can hardly wait to tell our friends. We'll be back!"

The restaurant had *credibility*. The people who came thought it offered a more-than-credible eating experience. Those who told their friends lent their credibility to the establishment as well.

Then something happened that was fortunate in some ways and unfortunate in others.

A well-known restaurant critic, who was a reporter for the evening news in Los Angeles on one of the major network television stations, was invited to visit the restaurant.

When he went, he experienced what everyone else did. It was a delightful restaurant. From the time he walked in, everything was perfect, from the courteous nature of the maître d', the staff, and the waiters to the inviting ambiance and cuisine.

He could hardly wait not only to tell his friends about it but also to do a program on it on the network affiliate in Los Angeles. The next night he was on the air. He was glowing with excitement about his newly found treasure, this place everyone should go to. He described the perfect little restaurant for the viewers: "Nothing there is hurried; everything is relaxed and wonderful. The food is delicious, the staff is courteous, and the ambiance is perfect. It's an ideal place to go with a date, by yourself —anytime you want to enjoy a wonderful culinary experience, this is the place!"

You guessed it. The next night, there were cars congested in a four-block area from all over the Los Angeles basin trying to get to this little restaurant. The cooks quickly ran out of food, which made the staff short tempered. Customers pressed the maître d' to let them slip into the line, flashing bills of attractive denominations as incentive. The servers became tired and discourteous. The food was prepared more quickly than usual, so it didn't taste quite as good as on the nights before.

This went on for about a week, and finally the restaurant owner just closed the doors, saying, "We cannot cope with it. We have no interest in coping with it. We are closed."

It is a timeless principle of life and of business:

If your visibility exceeds your ability, it will destroy your credibility!

Problem solving strengthens your ability. As your visibility grows, if your ability keeps pace, your credibility will allow organizational growth. But if you set goals in terms of visibility without problem solvers to strengthen your ability, every time you become visible and can't perform, you lose credibility, and your growth stops for a while.

PROBLEM SOLVERS FREQUENTLY END UP BRINGING VERY INNOVATIVE SOLUTIONS!

"Creativity is being demanded of managers not just in the context of what they do but in the process of how they get it done," says John Kao, Ph.D., an associate professor at Harvard Business School who teaches a course called "Entrepreneurship, Creativity, and Organization." . . .

Apparently corporate America agrees. In recent years, more than half of the Fortune 500 companies have adopted formal creativity-training programs for their employees. Such training can cost up to $500,000, but that's not stopping Proctor & Gamble, Best Foods, Kimberly-Clark, IBM, and others from eagerly signing on. . . .

The use of analogies also helped a farm-products company that was searching for a way to make sure its seeds would be planted with the proper amount of space in between, says Stanley S. Gryskiewicz, a group director at the Center for Creative Leadership in Greensboro, North Carolina. During the creative process, someone thought of a machine-gun ammunition belt. That did the trick: The am-

munition belt ultimately led to the idea of a roll of biode-
gradable tape studded with carefully spaced seeds that
could be laid along a furrow.[2]

Another example comes from a very familiar name.

KRAFT, A FORMER GROCER CLERK, KNEW ABOUT THE PROBLEMS

Cheese hardly seemed like a promising product to build a
new business around when James L. Kraft (1874–1953)
began wholesaling it to Chicago grocery stores in 1904.
Americans ate little cheese, and the biggest problem stand-
ing in the way of increased sales was spoilage. Cheese had
a very short shelf life and so was regarded suspiciously by
both consumers and store owners. . . .

Kraft, a former grocer clerk, knew about the problems
but was convinced that he could reach a larger market by
packaging cheese in more convenient, less perishable
forms. He started his business (now Kraft Cheese) by sell-
ing small individual portions of cheese in glass jars and
tinfoil packages. These were major improvements, but there
was still the tendency of cheese to spoil too quickly.

In 1916, Kraft solved the spoilage problem by patenting
a method of blending, pasteurizing, and packaging Ameri-
can cheddar that dramatically increased the cheese's shelf
life. Packed in four-ounce tins, the new "processed cheese"
retained its freshness and flavor over long periods.

Further refinements made it possible for Kraft to substi-
tute foil-wrap packaging for the heavier and less efficient
tins. This paved the way for the arrival of the company's
famous five-pound cheeseloaf.[3]

Problem solving can actually be a part of a person's position description.

Quad/Graphics is one of the nation's leading printing companies and prints national magazines, such as *People* and *Sports Illustrated*. It has described nine roles and responsibilities for its customer service representatives, including Planner, Problem Solver, Scheduler, and Communicator. Problem solving is a defined role and responsibility.

Quality (the result of problem solving) is often a part of an organization's official values statement. Many organizations have mission statements or philosophy statements or statements of quality emphasis.

AT&T, in its Quality Policy, says that every employee is part of the quality system, and "each of us will strive to identify and eliminate the sources of error and waste in our processes and procedures. . . . Each of us will aid the quality planning and improvement efforts of others for the good of the corporation as a whole."

Part of the Madison, Wisconsin, Police Department's quality statement says, "We believe in empowering employees to implement solutions to customer-identified problems."

8

Identify the Goal Setters and the Problem Solvers on Your Team

Wise team leaders take the time to study their team members and to analyze their goal-versus-problem orientation. The following inventory might allow you to understand your team members better by helping you determine whether each person on your team is a goal setter or a problem solver.

STAFF ASSESSMENT PROFILE

Staff member's name _____

(On each row, check the box on the left or the right that you think most nearly reflects the thoughts, feelings, or preferences of the staff person.)

GOAL SETTER'S STRENGTHS	PROBLEM SOLVER'S STRENGTHS
☐ I love setting goals, and it is emotionally very satisfying each and every time I reach a goal I have set.	☐ I love solving problems, and it is very emotionally satisfying every time I solve a problem no one else could solve.
☐ I keep going over and over my goals. I keep track of the big picture, possibly forgetting problems.	☐ I lose track of or forget goals, but I keep tightly focused on problems.
☐ Most people think of me as an extremely positive and optimistic goal setter, although I appear to some as unrealistic.	☐ I see myself as an extremely positive and optimistic problem solver, although some people misread me and think of me as negative.
☐ I am basically a risk taker once the goal is clearly defined.	☐ I will take some risks, but only after careful research has been completed and the potential problems have been carefully identified.
☐ I am continually seeking a new and different goal.	☐ I tend to stay with the tried and true, the proven, solid successes.

☐ I find a clearly defined goal energizing.	☐ I find a good, hard problem energizing.
☐ I am "hard to guard" when going for one of life's "goal lines" to score points!	☐ No one gets around me. I can ask enough tough questions to stop poorly developed ideas.
☐ I identify more with the Marines: Bomb the bridge and take the beachhead!	☐ I identify more with the Army Corps of Engineers: Rebuild the bombed-out bridge and reconstruct the beach.
☐ I go for the gold!	☐ I go for the gold—after I make sure we don't lose the gold we already have!

GOAL SETTER'S STRUGGLES	PROBLEM SOLVER'S STRUGGLES
☐ I sometimes have trouble seeing and dealing with obvious problems and being patient with all the seemingly negative questions problem solvers ask.	☐ Sometimes I find it difficult to keep the big picture in view. I tend to get lost in the details of a project or a problem.

☐ I get bored rather easily and constantly need new goals to keep me challenged.	☐ I am somewhat uncomfortable with new goals, especially when there are no proven models or in situations I have never seen before.
☐ I dislike and tend to put off detailed follow-through and prefer heading toward my next big goal.	☐ I frequently find it difficult to face new situations. I distrust my own instincts when I am in a new situation.

TYPE OF SUPERVISION GOAL SETTER PREFERS	TYPE OF SUPERVISION PROBLEM SOLVER PREFERS
☐ I really need to have clear goals and to be given the resources and the freedom to reach them.	☐ I prefer being assigned specific problems that have stumped everyone else for some time and then solve them.
☐ I need to keep my goals visible and constantly carry with me a list of the goals I am working on.	☐ I keep a list of problems with me all of the time and look at them frequently throughout the week.
☐ I celebrate goals reached far more than I do problems solved.	☐ I celebrate problems solved far more than I do goals reached.

THE QUESTION THAT'S USUALLY IN MY MIND WHEN I'M AROUND A PROBLEM SOLVER	THE QUESTION THAT'S USUALLY IN MY MIND WHEN I'M AROUND A GOAL SETTER
☐ "Why are you always so negative?"	☐ "Why set new goals when you didn't follow through on the ones you set last year?"

TOTAL POINTS: ___ Goal Setter ___ Problem Solver

BOTTOM LINE—I SEE MY STAFF PERSON AS A:

_____

_____

You may want to create a grid like the one that follows. It will help you keep track of which staff members prefer goal setting and which prefer problems. Then you can make assignments accordingly.

STAFF MEMBERS	GOALS	PROBLEMS
J. IRA	X	
KIMBERLY B.		X
CHERYL	X	
JOLI		X
JAMI	X	
JENNY		X
KIMBERLY K.	X	

UNDERSTANDING, LEADING, AND MAXIMIZING PROBLEM SOLVERS

As a problem solver you have, more than likely, experienced a situation similar to the one I'm about to describe. It is a basic dynamic between goal setters and problem solvers, and I have seen it repeated again and again in the past twenty-five years.

1. A goal setter comes up with a "brand spanking new" idea.
2. He or she presents the idea to the problem solver in its raw form.
3. The problem solver asks such hard, tough, challenging questions that the goal setter feels "blown out of the water."
4. The goal setter decides never to share a new idea with the problem solver again because the problem solver is "so negative."

That scenario can be avoided with some minor changes in presentation. There is a step-by-step process you can use starting today. It is profoundly simple and very practical, and it works like this:

1. The goal setter comes up with a new idea.
2. The goal setter alerts the problem solver to be in a *brainstorming mode,* not a *decision-making mode.* (Problem solvers tend to assume, whenever an idea comes up, that the goal setter is trying to make a decision and is about to "bet the farm on a half-baked idea.")

3. After it is clear that they are in a brainstorming mode, the goal setter presents the idea. (Problem solvers are comfortable brainstorming for a long time, as long as the ground rules are clear. They will stay in a brainstorming mode until the goal setter begins to take some action indicating he or she is about to make a decision. At that point, they ask the appropriately tough questions.)
4. Once the brainstorming phase has been completed, the goal setter gives the problem solver a verbal alert that they are shifting into the decision-making mode. The tough questions that the problem solver asks will result in a wiser decision.

Both goal setters and problem solvers should take the initiative to clarify whether they are in a brainstorming or decision-making mode. (Ideas will be far better received if they do.) Anyone can easily stop the conversation before it gets more than a sentence old and ask a simple clarifying question:

"Are we brainstorming or deciding?"

Once that is clear, regardless of who takes the initiative to clarify the agenda, the communication between goal setters and problem solvers will be a whole lot smoother!

Before goal setters make a major commitment of important resources, they should get problem solvers' wisdom on their side. Before your friend invests hard-earned dollars, it is important for you to help by asking tough decision-making questions. (You might want to add some questions from Appendix A to your decision-making questions.) You need to know what problems you will face before you finally say, "Go!"

There are times when you need to be asking brainstorming questions. At other times, it is appropriate to ask expansion, refining, or control questions. The following grid will help you see clearly the phases of an idea and the type of questions that should be asked in each phase.

Staff Member's Role Preference	Designer	Designer-Developer	Developer	Developer-Maintainer	Maintainer
Predictable reaction to new ideas	Gets excited about new theory	Excited, expands, dreams, sees great potential	Asks for two or three proven models and a clear goal, then gets excited	Is cautious, suffers paralysis-by-analysis, asks hard questions too soon in the process	Finds new ideas very stressful
What needs to be done in this phase	Define the theory	Build a prototype	Roll out the model	Refine the systems	Maintain control
Emotional reaction to new ideas	Excited	Excited	Eager	Cautious	Stressed
Type of question to ask in this phase	Brainstorming	Brainstorming, some realistic	Expansion	Refining	Control

TEN QUESTIONS FOR A PROBLEM SOLVER TO ASK IN THE EARLY STAGES OF AN IDEA

1. Are we brainstorming, or are we trying to decide whether to invest our money?
2. How long do we have before we need to make a final decision?
3. What brainstorming questions should we be asking? (See Appendix A.)
4. Does anyone mind if I start a list of questions we need to ask later?
5. Does anyone mind if I just listen for a while until the idea is a little more developed?
6. What advantages would there be to our organization, and to our division, if this idea were really successful?
7. What three things do I like about this new idea? What do I like best about it?
8. Who would be the very best person to lead this program?
9. Am I being overly cautious? Am I the only one seeing the potentially dangerous problems I am seeing? Am I learning by watching what's going on here?
10. How can I encourage the leaders before I start asking the harder questions?

For you as a problem solver, it is important to realize that in a start-up phase, goals are necessary. When nothing exists to refine, someone needs to set some goals. You need goal setters to set goals. After a successful start-up, when the organization is on the move, it is wise to move to more of a balance of goal setters and problem solvers.

If you are a problem solver involved in (stuck in) a start-up phase, you will likely find it very stressful. If you need clarification of longer-term direction, ask the team to state what they want in place ten years from now. Then you can begin to define problems that will need to be solved to get there.

A REALISTIC PROBLEM SOLVING PROCESS

What problem are you facing head-on? If you and I were on a deserted island for a month to talk about any subject you chose, what problem would you want to discuss? If I could solve one problem for you and you knew for sure that it would be solved, what would you most want solved?

Henry Ford is credited with having said, "Most people spend more time and energy in going around problems than in trying to solve them."

Stop reading for a moment. Decide which problem you need or want to solve. Then use the grid on pages 132 and 133 to help you solve the problem.

The problem I most need or want to solve today is:

_____.

In the future, whenever you face a problem, I hope following this simple, proven process will be as helpful to you as it has been to our team. I first introduced it at one of our consulting schools back in 1985. Since then, our team has helped many clients by following the process in a step-by-step manner.

Claude Robold, a consulting associate with Master-planning Group and the president of Mentoring Today, has probably used this problem-solving process the most in his work. He comments:

> The greatest loss one can suffer is the loss of hope. The difference in someone solving a critical problem—whether it be a tragedy, crisis, or personal failure—is whether they are able to maintain hope. Having a process for solving life's problems always offers hope. Where there is help, there is hope.

KEY WORD	ACTION STEP	PROFOUND QUESTION	PRIMARY PRINCIPLE
PERSONAL	Check your personal balance.	How is my personal balance, or imbalance, affecting my perceptions?	An imbalanced person tends to make unwise, expedient decisions.
PRIORITIZE	Make a ninety-day to-do list for priority problems.	What is the single most important priority problem?	Deal with prioritized problems *one at a time!*
CONTEXT	Contextualize the number-one problem.	What is the appropriate context (typically a process) for this problem?	Nothing is meaningful without a context.

CAUSE	Isolate the cause of the problem.	What is the central cause of the problem or roadblock?	Focus your attention on causes, not symptoms. Ignore symptoms as much as possible.
OPTIONS	Brainstorm options to solve the problem.	What are my options?	The more options the better—at first.
DECIDE	Decide which option is best.	Of my top two to five options, which is best?	Avoid "choosing" from one option.
ACT	Start, and move toward the goal.	How can I become more effective and more efficient? How can I move toward the ideal?	When you are doing something another person could do 80 percent as well, you may be wasting your time. Delegate!
MARK	Mark your trail for the next time you encounter a similar problem.	What did I learn in dealing with this problem?	Never re-invent the wheel, but never stop refining the tire!

Claude Robold adds, "I believe that problem solving brings to an individual the understanding that he is capable of making healthy decisions. We often forget we are fearfully and wonderfully made and therefore succumb to the idea that we are incapable of making decisions. As we solve problems, we are building confidence in our decision-making ability."

If you haven't done so already, take a few minutes right now to use the grid to help bring perspective to the problem that you indicated you wanted to solve.

UNDERSTANDING, LEADING, AND MAXIMIZING GOAL SETTERS

As a problem solver, it is critical for you to learn to work with and to maximize the strengths of goal setters. You need to be able to bring up problems you see without setting off World War III. The goal setter you most need to understand and work with might be your team leader, your spouse, your business partner, or your child. Regardless, you need goal setters!

Goal setters are basically future-oriented people. Goal setters are as interested in the dream of what life will be like after their goals have been met as you are in the realities of today.

Whenever you are working with a goal setter, the first thing to remember is which of the *five developmental phases* your project is in.

DESIGN	DESIGN-DEVELOPMENT	DEVELOPMENT	DEVELOPMENT-MAINTENANCE	MAINTENANCE

Always remember the grid. It will help keep the perspective of goal setters clear in your mind.

Staff Member's Role Preference	Designer	Designer-Developer	Developer	Developer-Maintainer	Maintainer
Predictable reaction to new ideas	Gets excited about new theory	Excited, expands, dreams, sees great potential	Asks for two or three proven models and a clear goal, then gets excited	Is cautious, suffers paralysis-by-analysis, asks hard questions too soon in the process	Finds new ideas very stressful
What needs to be done in this phase	Define the theory	Build a prototype	Roll out the model	Refine the systems	Maintain control
Type of question to ask in this phase	Brainstorming	Brainstorming, some realistic	Expansion	Refining	Control
Key word in this phase	Patience	Patience	Patience	Patience	Patience

In the design phase of a project, you need a theory-oriented problem solver. In the maintenance phase you need a prevention-oriented problem solver. You need to know what phase a project is in before you really know if you need a goal setter or a problem solver.

The second thing to remember is to *praise* the idea and the plan if at all possible before you point out the problems. The third thing to remember is to come up with *two or three alternative solutions,* if possible, to every problem you point out.

PUTTING TOGETHER A PRACTICAL PLAN WITHOUT A SINGLE GOAL

When it comes to establishing a clear plan for an organization or a project, I've seen a few emotional reactions many times. Do any of them sound familiar?

"Goals Equal Failure to Me"

One typical response to the process of planning goes something like this: "Does that have anything to do with goals? If it has anything to do with goals, I don't want any part of it because every time I've set goals in the past, I've failed." In my experience, problem solvers do not get frustrated with planning; it is goal setting that is the problem.

If you happen to be in a work situation where you are forced to set goals, set realistic goals, not pie-in-the-sky goals. The point is not to impress people with the goals you set but to set realistic, measurable goals.

"I'm Just Not Good at Planning"

Frankly, most people aren't good at planning. That's because they have never really been taught how to plan. On the following pages you will learn a simple, step-by-step planning process that will work for any organization, no matter the size, and you will never have to set a single goal. If you are still uneasy in the planning process, you might want to try writing out your plan by yourself. Write out your plan, following the process I suggest, but don't show it to anyone, or plan to show it to anyone, until you are 100 percent comfortable with it. When you are, then make it public.

"Who Really Knows What Will Happen Two to Twenty Years from Now?"

Some people object to long-range planning because no one really knows what will happen years from now. I'll develop this in more detail later, but for now keep in mind that the primary purpose of long-range (five, ten, or twenty years) planning is to get your team headed in the same basic direction. You may never actually accomplish all the priorities you establish; the important thing is that you are headed in the right direction.

The chances of reaching all of your twenty-year goals are probably about 10 percent. There is *no* realistic chance of reaching 100 percent of them. But if the members of your team are all headed in the right direction today, they are indeed working as a *team* rather than as individuals going in different directions.

MAJOR BENEFITS OF HAVING A CLEAR PLAN FOR THE FUTURE

In this section, we'll discuss making one of the most critical, sometimes frightening, but often satisfying moves in all of leadership—from response to initiation. Having confidence to make the move from responding to initiating is one benefit of having a clear plan for the future.

A second benefit a clear plan provides is a better context for wise decision making. For example, once you decide whether you are going to keep growing or level out for a year or two, you know the building size you are going to need.

A third benefit is increased motivation. When you are coming out of a fog, so to speak, it tends to get exciting. Be the person who creates an island of clarity in a sea of confusion. At work, for instance, you might be saying to yourself, "This place is a mess! No one knows what he is doing. There is a sea of confusion around here."

> **Be the person who creates an island of clarity in a sea of confusion.**

Do what you are supposed to do regardless of whether your team leader does, your staff does, or your peers do. Begin to create an island of clarity in a sea of confusion. It doesn't matter if no other leader in your department, division, or company has a clear plan. Once you develop a clear plan that your staff agrees with 100 percent, you will find that it unlocks natural motivation, team spirit, and excitement about the future.

The fourth benefit of having a clear plan in place is that you can re-focus anytime in ten to thirty minutes, and you never have to start over. I'll never forget an experience I had nearly thirty years ago in South Bend, Indiana. I was sitting on a park bench, overlooking the St. Joseph river across the road from the South Bend campus of Indiana University. It was the kind of spring day that made everything seem possible. The sky was blue. The clouds were white. The breeze was blowing gently. Life seemed somewhat predictable and under control.

"Well, I should develop a plan for my future today," I thought. So on the back side of an envelope, I promptly spelled out what I hoped would be my future.

Would it be difficult for you to guess what I found in the bottom of a drawer three years later? How many times do we put together a plan and then forget the plan? When you've forgotten the plan, or when you've lost track of the plan, you will feel as if you've never had a plan. You think, *I'm as foggy as I've ever been*.

But once your plans are in written form, the furthest you are from focus is ten to thirty minutes. Simply take out your plans again, and my prediction is that you will think to yourself, "I have made a lot more progress than I thought I had!" Once you get draft one done, you never have to start over. You never have to reinvent the wheel; you just keep refining the tire.

They say a cat always lands on its feet. Did you ever see those commercials where they drop a cat out of a two-story building, and they show, in slow motion, how the cat turns around? What happens if you lay a cat on its back and put all its feet in the air and just take your hands out from under it? The cat starts on its back, but the first thing it does is to get its head straight. It basically turns its head, leaving its feet in the air, and looks at the ground. The cat's body responds quickly, but only after the cat has gotten its head straight.

THE WAY TO ALWAYS "LAND ON YOUR FEET" IN LEADERSHIP IS TO GET YOUR HEAD STRAIGHT FIRST

Once you understand the process of planning a team's direction, you can land on your feet as a leader anywhere, at any time, for the rest of your life. And that's important. If you serve on any kind of board—an alumni board at your school, your family's business board, or a corporation's board of directors—one thing you want to be able to do at any point is to get your head straight and land on your feet.

THE MASTERPLANNING ARROW

Have you ever struggled for a long time with a problem and found that when the answer finally came, it had a far wider application than just your current problem?

The idea for the Masterplanning Arrow (a poster-sized planning sheet) came out of an assignment I had back in 1980.

My wife, Cheryl, and I were working on the planning process late into the night. At about 2:00 A.M., it occurred to me that if we had a big enough sheet of paper, we could display the direction of the entire organization on a single sheet for everyone on the board to see. I began sketching it out, and the Masterplanning Arrow was born. Since then, the Masterplanning Arrow has gone through five or six fairly major revisions.

Today, several hundred organizations have adopted it as one of their official planning tools, and literally thousands of leaders have learned to communicate their group's future direction using the Masterplanning Arrow.

The Masterplanning Arrow is used daily by presidents of major corporations, pastors of local churches, and leaders starting their own organizations. It is a lifelong tool. No matter what you're ever asked to plan, you can use the Masterplanning Arrow to help clarify your group's basic direction.

track + action = traction

A *track* is a plan for the future you face. The *Masterplanning Arrow* is one proven way to define your track into the future, for your team to follow.

Some people are good at taking action, but they have no real plan or track, so they spin their wheels. Other people are good at making plans, but they never act! Therefore, they have no *traction*.

When your team has a clear *track* and takes *action*, you get *traction* to take you from where you are to where you want to go! So let's begin.

1. NEEDS

Just under the heavy line, you will see some numbers. Over on the right-hand side are listed:

1. NEEDS
2. PURPOSE
3. OBJECTIVES

MASTERPLANNING

	4. MILESTONES What major mile-stones have we already accomplished? (Transitional, funda-mental, measurable.)	5. IDEAS What ideas have we had that we should consider turning into goals in the future? (Current high potential thoughts, possibilities.)	6. ROADBLOCKS What is keeping us from reaching our full potential? (Specific, major, current.)	7. RESOURCES What are our greatest resources? (Specific, major, current.)	8. QUARTERLY GOALS/PROBLEMS In the next 90 days, what are our specific measurable, targets of accomplishment? (Specific, realistic, measurable.)	9. SHORT RANG GOALS/PROE In the next 0-2 what are our s measurable, t of accomplish (Specific, realis measurable.)
1.						
2.						
3.						
4.						
5.						
6.						
7.						
8.						

ARROW

MID-RANGE GOALS/PROBLEMS	11. LONG-RANGE GOALS/PROBLEMS	3. OBJECTIVES	2. PURPOSE	1. NEEDS
In the next 2-5 years, what are our possible targets of accomplishment? (General, yet measurable.)	In the next 5-20 years, what are we dreaming of accomplishing? (Broad brush, measurable.)	In what 3-7 areas will we continue being actively involved in the future? (Broad categories, nonmeasurable, continuous.)	**Why do we exist?** (Directional, umbrella statement, lifetime) **2A. PRIMARY RESULT** What is the best single measurable indicator of the health of our total organization?	**What needs do we feel deeply burdened by and uniquely qualified to meet?** **What makes us weep or pound the table?** (Categorically specific, emotional, continuous.)

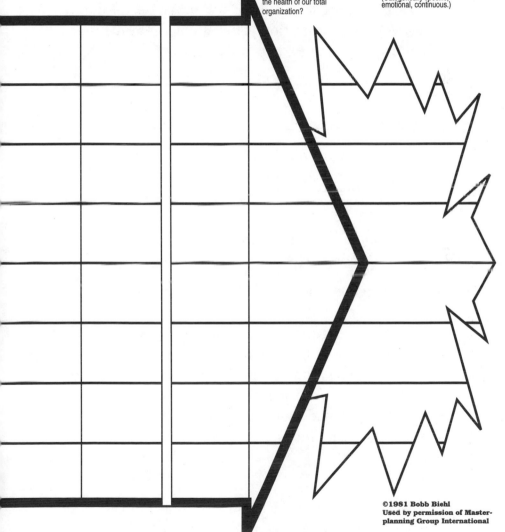

©1981 Bobb Biehl
Used by permission of Masterplanning Group International

The numbers represent the sequence you follow to fill out your *Masterplanning Arrow*.

The "Needs" section is where you want to invest a considerable amount of time making sure your group is in complete agreement on the needs you'll meet and the purpose or reason for meeting them. These needs are *outside* of your organization. They are *not* internal items such as copy machines, paper, or desks.

Step 1

The question is:

What needs does our team feel deeply burdened by and uniquely qualified to meet?

Next ask:

What makes us weep or pound the table?

Another way to ask this question is: "What are we deeply concerned about? What would we give our money to?"

Needs are categorically specific. For example: "We care for all teenage girls" is a very wide, general statement of concern. A more specific identification would be, "We have a concern for unwed teenage mothers." This is still a broad statement, but it is considerably more specific in its focus.

Step 2

You may feel burdened by many things and wonder how to distinguish between those you should address and those you shouldn't address. That's why the second part of the question is so important:

What needs does our team feel deeply burdened by and uniquely qualified to meet?

Which of the needs you feel deeply burdened by is your team *uniquely qualified* to meet?

2. PURPOSE

The next step in the process is to define your purpose. Purpose is a single statement of why a team or an organization exists. The question to ask to determine purpose is:

In the light of all the needs we see, why do we exist as an organization?

A purpose statement is your North Star. The North Star is not a place you go; it's a fixed point that gives you perspective on where you are going. Your purpose statement keeps you headed in the right general direction.

A purpose statement is a specific umbrella statement explaining why you do everything you do within your organization.

Defining your purpose might require several hours, several days, or several drafts. Some groups have taken a full day just to write a one-sentence purpose statement. They hammered and chipped and chiseled at it until everyone felt 100 percent comfortable with the placement of every word.

An easy way to define your group's purpose is to work through the following steps:

Step 1

Ask your team this question:

What single, solitary word describes the focus of our organization?

The word is not a purpose statement, but it should represent the single focus within your organization (profit, service, sales, people).

Step 2

After you have the single-word focus, the next step is to ask:

What two or three words would explain why we exist?

Step 3

Put your two or three words into a single, nontechnical phrase or sentence that anyone could easily understand.

Develop your purpose statement to a "party level." If you met someone for the first time at a party, and in making polite conversation the person asked what your organization is all about, what one phrase or sentence would you use to sum up your organization's purpose in a simple, easy-to-understand way?

Your purpose might be as simple as:

To maximize Junior League leadership in Orange County, Florida.

That's why your organization exists. That's what you tell people at parties. That's what you tell people on airplanes. It's simple, and it's clear. That's a "party level" purpose statement. At the same time it gives your team members a profoundly simple focus for everything they do, day in and day out.

If you need more help to clarify your team's purpose, try these questions:

How are we unique among all other groups and organizations?

What five to ten fundamental assumptions do we make about ourselves?

Often, spelling out assumptions helps to clarify your uniqueness.

One additional thought: A purpose statement (personal or organizational) is actually an epitaph in present tense. What would you want your epitaph (personal or organizational) to read some day? Your ideal epitaph can provide a profoundly simple insight into your purpose for existing today.

For example, missionary and education pioneer Frank Laubach's epitaph read, "He taught the world to read." During his life, his purpose statement could have been "To teach the world to read."

3. OBJECTIVES

Purpose is a single statement of why a team or organization exists. Objectives are the general areas (called objective areas) in which your effort is directed.

Ask yourself this question:

In what three to seven areas will we continue to be actively involved in the future?

In other words, "What are we going to do?" You are looking for broad categories. Objectives are non-measurable, undated, and ongoing. Objectives are not meant to be measurable. *Always list objectives alphabetically to avoid unintentionally insulting the department that is listed last.*

A few examples of objectives (all of these lists are stated with an intentionally simple style for clarity of communication) on a business *Masterplanning Arrow* might be:

- To continue providing engineering services
- To continue providing international support services
- To provide manufacturing
- To provide operational/administrative support
- To continue providing sales and marketing support
- To continue providing transportation services

One of the best ways to tell whether an area is clearly defined and objective is to ask, "Could I assign a person to be responsible for this area of activity?" For example, could you ask a person to be responsible for all of the transportation in the organization? Yes. For manufacturing? Yes. If you can assign a person, on a continuing basis, to be responsible for everything going on in an area, it is probably a clear, objective area.

4. MILESTONES

In each objective area, what are the major milestones you've already reached? These are turning-point milestones, things that were significant to your organization's development.

For example: You introduced a new curriculum, you hired a new director, you dedicated a new building, you hosted a convention, or you initiated a training program.

What are the milestones we've already reached?

Typically only milestones attained in the last two years would go on your *Masterplanning Arrow.* You might want to indicate near each milestone the date on which it was reached.

Writing milestones down is recording history. When you bring in new board members or hire new staff members and are orienting them, you can say, "This is our purpose, these are our objectives, and here are some of our milestones."

Another reason for recording milestones is that they are a "pocketful of sunshine for a rainy day." When you feel discouraged, you can remember what you and your team have already accomplished.

The "Milestones" section of your *Masterplanning Arrow* is a time for celebration, so just have a good time remembering, as a group, all of your past accomplishments.

5. IDEAS

Ask yourself:

What ideas do we have that we should consider making priorities?

These ideas are possible solutions to the problems you see. They are possibilities.

Never Lose a Good Idea!

How many times have you seen someone make a zillion dollars on an idea, and you think to yourself, "I thought of that idea years ago! If only I'd done something about it!" Many potentially great ideas are lost to humnankind because they are not written down. Never lose a good idea! Always have a place to file ideas.

Don't Confuse Ideas with Priorities

Be careful not to confuse your ideas with your priorities, which we'll cover later. If you look at every idea as a priority you've set, you will end up spreading your energies in so many directions you won't accomplish anything. Part of the beauty of the *Masterplanning Arrow* is that it helps you distinguish between your ideas for the future and the priorities you will actually pursue in the present.

6. ROADBLOCKS

One question every leader should be continually asking is:

What three major roadblocks (megaproblems) are keeping us from reaching our priorities (in each of our objective areas)?

Whatever you're leading, whether it's your own company, a university, a battalion in the military, or a small department, you want to be fully aware of your three main roadblocks at all times.

Typically, roadblocks are specific, current, major areas of blockage. List your top three roadblocks for each objective category.

As a leader, you cannot focus on getting rid of all your roadblocks at once. You need to narrow it down to a few strategic targets.

Prediction

As you list your top three roadblocks for each objective category, you'll begin to see patterns develop. Often the same roadblock exists in several objective areas. That implies that a leadership team needs to focus on removing those roadblocks, which are holding the whole organization back. Common roadblocks are a lack of capital (money) and the need to train leadership. A leadership team facing those problems needs to focus on how to generate the income required and how to train the leadership required to accomplish its priorities.

7. RESOURCES

Now list the resources you have available. Ask:

What are our three greatest resources in each objective area?

These are specific, major, current resources.

In the recent history of leadership development, the emphasis has been: "Focus on overcoming your weaknesses." My personal counsel is to spend 95 percent of your time maximizing your strengths (resources) and 5 percent overcoming your weaknesses.

List your top three resources in each objective area. Just as you found patterns of weakness with all of your roadblocks, so also you'll find patterns of strength in your resources.

8. PRIORITIES

A priority can be a goal or a problem. It is a realistic, measurable, dated target of accomplishment in the future.

I've come to the conclusion that a man doesn't need priorities if he has no dreams. But if he has dreams and no priorities . . . he has only despair!
—Bill Owen, President
Decision Support Unlimited
Yorba Linda, California

The statement by Bill Owen captures the essence of why establishing priorities is so critical. I have talked with many leaders who have grand dreams but no bridge to get there, and they actually feel great sadness and despair.

Basically, priorities are like a stairway to your dreams. Priorities become the bridge to turn your dreams into reality.

Nothing Is Meaningful without a Context

One of the reasons why people fail in establishing realistic priorities is that they haven't established the proper context. What you have done so far on your *Masterplanning Arrow* establishes that context. Once you know:

- the needs you're trying to meet;
- your purpose in trying to meet them;
- your objectives (the categories in which you will be working);
- the milestones you've already reached;
- your very best ideas; and
- your resources and your roadblocks,

you've established the context that makes establishing realistic priorities possible.

Let's look at what priorities should be.

Priorities Must Be Measurable

First, priorities must be measurable, or they're only good intentions. A poor example would be: "My priority is to do better next year." That is not a measurable priority. It's simply a good intention.

Priorities Should Be Written in Pencil

Second, priorities should always be written in pencil, or else they become concrete boxes and can be used as whips. Bill Owen also said, "Priorities should be in sand. . . . And our purpose in concrete. . . . Not the other way around."

Another reason why priorities should be written in pencil is that nobody knows what's going to happen tomorrow. An ancient Chinese proverb says, "He who would know the future three days in advance, his family would be wealthy for generations!" The economy may fall or surge. Priorities are based on today, and they may need to change tomorrow.

Priorities Must Be Realistic

Third, priorities have to be realistic, or they are a setup for failure. Have you ever wondered why people typically establish unrealistic priorities and then feel like failures when they don't achieve them all?

Here are a few of the most common reasons:

People establish priorities when they are emotionally excited. Priorities set during such times tend to be unrealistic. Wait to establish your priorities until you're at a balanced emotional state.

People establish priorities when they have no track record. If you have never milked a cow, don't brag about how many gallons you'll get the first time from those things hanging under the cow into that shiny new silver pail.

If you're going into a new situation, perhaps a new work assignment, ask the manager, "What has the average person done in this position before me?" Some managers, particularly in sales, tell you what the most successful person has done before. They don't tell you what the average person did. Ask for some kind of context or comparison so that you can set your goals within a realistic framework.

People want to please or impress their leaders. They may want to impress the manager, or the board, so they set extremely high priorities. But it's a short-lived victory when, six months later, the "super priorities" aren't reached and the overzealous workers look like failures to the very people they were trying so hard to impress.

If in the past the word *planning* has put an emotional knot in your stomach, let me suggest that you consider two guidelines:

1. Establish priorities you *know* you can accomplish.
2. Avoid establishing priorities in situations that are emotionally "Rah! Rah!" If you're forced to establish priorities in such a situation, ask for context so you know you've got a realistic reference point from which to set your priorities.

Now for some good news:

You don't have to reach every priority you establish to make a significant difference!

Don't look at your priorities as whips. Look at them as motivational targets and as exciting, measurable milestones for the future. If you don't reach them all, don't see yourself as a failure. In fact, if you reach 60 percent to 80 percent of your priorities for the year, consider yourself a major success!

Special Note

There are no commonly agreed upon time frames for short-, mid-, and long-range priorities. Your organization must decide on time frames that suit your team. You might decide that for your team, short-range will be one year, midrange two years, and long-range three years.

Short-Range Priorities

Skip the ninety-day priorities for now. We'll come back to them later. For short-range priorities, the question to ask is:

In the next zero to two years, what are our top three realistic, measurable targets of accomplishment for each objective area?

These should be very specific. Your short-range priorities become the foundation for your twenty-year dreams.

REALITY CHECK: Even as the president of a successful consulting firm that teaches planning, I would say there is only a 50 percent to 70 percent chance that your short-range priorities will happen as initially written.

People change, economies change, and communities change.

Set a maximum of three priorities per objective area. Frequently, people set far too many priorities and feel overshadowed and lost in their "forest of priorities."

Midrange Priorities

Midrange priorities are the same as short-range priorities, except the time frame is the next two to five years. The question to ask is:

In the next two to five years, what are our top three realistic, measurable targets of accomplishment for each objective area?

Midrange priorities will be a little more speculative and a bit more uncertain than short-range priorities, but still measurable.

Keep in mind that all priorities are flexible. As situations change, so may the timing of certain priorities. You can erase a short-range priority and make it a midrange priority, or vice versa, but basically everything can stay somewhere on your *Masterplanning Arrow*. Every great idea you have may become a milestone as it works its way to different parts of your *Arrow* at the appropriate time. The key is that no great idea is ever lost, only postponed until its proper time.

Long-Range Priorities

Thinking about your long-range priorities, the question to ask is:

What three realistic, measurable priorities for each objective area are we dreaming of accomplishing five to twenty years from now?

With a five- to twenty-year time frame, these are pie-in-the-sky priorities, but they still need to be stated in realistic, measurable terms.

The long-range priorities you set today have about a 10 percent chance of happening as originally written. Long-range planning is considered by some people to be a futile exercise. The purpose of looking this far ahead is to give your group a general sense of heading in the same direction. That will help you begin to make the same assumptions about the future and give you a context for making day-to-day decisions.

WARNING: As you think about possible long-range priorities, don't compare yourself with your past or your peers. Compare yourself with your own potential and the needs you see, to gain a clear vision for the future.

Relax and try to imagine for a few minutes what your life would be like if all your priorities could be met.

Quarterly (Ninety-Day) Priorities

With ninety-day priorities, all you're doing is looking at your short-, mid-, and long-range plans to decide what specific things you should be working on currently. Ask:

In the next ninety days, what are our top three realistic, measurable targets of accomplishment for each objective area?

As a leader, you want everyone reporting to you to know precisely what you're expecting of them. You also want to show them what you'll be doing in the next ninety days. Remember, these priorities are targets, not whips.

CONCLUSION

A very high percentage (possibly as high as 80 percent) of your success or failure as a leader will depend on your ability to help your team focus by creating a clear master plan. That can be accomplished by setting clear, realistic, and measurable goals to reach *or* by defining clear, realistic, and measurable problems to solve. Either way, you have a clear plan.

The *Masterplanning Arrow* gives you a context within which to establish those clear, realistic, measurable priorities. Once your *Masterplanning Arrow* is complete, a quick update every month or two can help keep your team's future in crystal-clear focus.

You are free to use the planning instructions I've given you without obtaining a *Masterplanning Arrow*. However, if you would like to see all of your plans on a single sheet of paper, you can obtain a *Masterplanning Arrow* by calling Masterplanning Group at our toll-free number: 1-800-969-1976.

A DREAM AND A NINETY-DAY FOCUS MAXIMIZE BOTH GOAL SETTERS AND PROBLEM SOLVERS

Over the past twenty years or so, I have consulted with over 150 clients in the United States and around the world. I have met personally with over 1,500 executives for extended sessions. I have met with dozens of boards. I have had eight books published. With all of that background in management and leadership, would you be interested in the first three things I would do if I took your place at work today?

1. I'd get to know the team. Who are the goal setters? Who are the problem solvers? What are the team members' role preferences? What are their dreams? I'd establish the trust of the team. Without trust, nothing happens.
2. I'd define a clear dream and a primary result, as we discussed in Chapter 7. I'd make sure each person has a crystal-clear answer to the question "What are the three measurable priorities we will accomplish in the next ninety days to make a 50 percent difference in where we will be twelve months from now?"
3. I'd ask each staff person to answer five questions approximately once a month:

   - What *problems* do you need my help to solve?
   - What *decisions* do you need from me?
   - What *plans* are you making that we haven't discussed?
   - What *progress* have you made?

- How are you doing *personally* on a scale of 1 to 100? Why?

Regardless of whether the team leader is a goal setter or a problem solver and regardless of whether the team member is a goal setter or a problem solver, those five questions need to be asked and answered on a regular basis. See Appendix F for further discussion of staff members reporting on their priorities (goals or problems).

9

Free All Those Around You to Be Who They Are

I believe one of the most frequent and dangerous assumptions parents make is, "My children are like me, or they will be when they grow up." Goal-setting parents raising problem-solving children (or vice versa) can be very trying unless the parents have eyes to see how the children differ from them, and allow the children the freedom to be who they are.

It would be a helpful exercise for you to ask your child who is active in sports, "Would you rather score points or keep someone else from scoring points?" If he or she says, "I would rather score points," assume temporarily (other indicators might suggest a different orientation) that your child is a goal setter.

If your child says, "I would rather keep someone else from scoring," then assume temporarily that he or she is a problem solver. When you are assigning projects to a goal setter (everything from homework to housework), simply say, "Let's set a goal of doing this by this Wednesday." If you are working with a problem solver, say, "We've got a problem. Could you help me solve this problem by Wednesday?"

Very quickly, you will begin to see that your child's natural energy is far greater if you are working within his or her comfort zone.

"BUT DAD, I LOVE STOPPING PEOPLE FROM SCORING POINTS!"

A few weeks ago I was in Tokyo, Japan. While there, I had a conversation with a friend.

He said to me, "Bobb, when you talked to us last week about goal setting and problem solving, explaining that our natural instincts lean one way or the other, it reminded me of a conversation that I had just last week with my nine year-old son, who is an avid soccer player.

"Growing up as a child, I was a 100 percent goal setter, and so I have encouraged my son to be a scoring player on his soccer team. Not long ago, he came home from a game and our conversation went like this:

" 'Dad, I love playing out in front of the goalie where no one can get past me.'

" 'Well, Son, you've also got to score points because that's what the game is all about.'

" 'Yeah, but Dad, I love stopping people from scoring points!'

" 'Yes, but it's not any fun to do that if you don't score points.'

" 'But Dad, I love keeping other people from scoring points!'

"As you were talking, Bobb, it clarified in my mind just how loudly my son had been saying, 'I'm a problem solver. I'm a defensive player.' Because of my own preferences for goal setting, I hadn't been listening to him. I just wanted to say thank you for helping me see my son in a much clearer light."

Whenever I lecture to a group where couples are present and I explain the basic differences between people who enjoy setting goals and people who enjoy solving problems, there are always a lot of aha-type looks and gestures in the room.

Couples can be married for twenty-five years or more and still not really understand the implications of their differences. I believe there is an unspoken question between couples: "Who is stronger—my mate or me? Who is more right? Who needs to grow up?"

Many people I speak to realize, some for the first time, that their mates are very strong and very mature but different in their basic preferences. The question is not Who is right and who is wrong? or Who is mature and who is immature? The question is How do we differ and how can we maximize those adult differences and use them to strengthen both of us?

My wife is a goal setter, and I'm a problem solver. I ask not "Who is right?" but "How can we maximize our complementary strengths?"

Help adult members of your family—your siblings, your spouse, and your older children—understand the implications of the fact that some of them are goal setters and some are problem solvers. Help them understand what energizes them and how to work with people who are different from them. Help them know how to see opposites as different but not less. Help them grow in their ability to develop a unified team to win their "championship."

Free all of your friends to be who they are with no pressure to be more like you.

IMPLICATIONS FOR PARENTING

Were your grandparents goal setters or problem solvers? Put "goal setter" or "problem solver" in the spaces below:

DAD'S DAD	DAD'S MOM	MOM'S DAD	MOM'S MOM

How did your grandparents' preferences affect your parents?

Were your parents goal setters or problem solvers?

BIRTH MOM	BIRTH DAD	ADOPTED MOM	ADOPTED DAD

How did your parents' preferences affect you?

How about your brothers and sisters? Are they goal setters or problem solvers? Write their names in the top row; then write "goal setter" or "problem solver" in the corresponding spaces below each name.

How did your siblings' preferences affect you?
Are your children goal setters or problem solvers?

How do your children's preferences affect their relationship with you?

While talking with senior leaders around the world, I find that one common dynamic is the fact that a lot of their parents did not get along very well with their grandparents. That created a tense environment for their parents, which they have kept as a style of relating to the people. They say, "How could my parents have been any different, considering the home in which they were raised?"

A problem that few of our grandparents understood is the basic difference between goal setting and problem solving as it applied to their children. Therefore, they may have created an environment in which our parents who were goal setters were often treated like problem solvers because their parents were, or vice versa, thus creating a tremendous amount of frustration, pressure, and tension.

If your grandparents didn't understand the distinction, your parents may have the same similar assumption: "My children are like me, or they will be when they grow up." As I've already indicated, that is a fundamentally dangerous assumption, but it's common in our parents' generation.

As I work with groups, talking on the subject of manhood, about 30 percent of the men admit that they struggle with the issue of manhood: What is a man? When do you become a man? How do you know you are a man? and so on. I was watching a television interview one night, and the well-known host was interviewing a famous male movie star. The interviewer said, "You're a man. You're a man's man. You're a macho man. When does a man become a man?"

The star paused for a minute, and then he smiled the broad mustached smile that made him famous and said, "A man becomes a man when his daddy tells him he is, and not until."

I thought to myself that evening, *You old fox! You're smarter than I thought you looked in your movies. That was a pretty insightful answer.*

However, about three months later, that answer exploded in my brain because I thought, *Oh, no. If he's right, we're all in trouble because of the number of men whose parents have left home, have died, have divorced, have run away, or have in some other way become unavailable.*

And then I began thinking of a number of men whose dads never told them that they were men. I began seeing a whole new dynamic. Perhaps one reason why fathers do not tell their sons they are men is that their sons haven't become like them yet.

Let's say, for example, you're a farmer, and your son is a fine artist. He may grow up to be far more famous than Picasso, van Gogh, and Michelangelo, but if he doesn't milk forty cows in the morning before breakfast, you may wonder, *Is he a real man yet? Because he's certainly not like me. He's not making a living with his hands. He's not doing what I know manhood to be.*

The point is, of course, that parents should take into account the goal setter–problem solver distinction when assessing the maturity of their children. Children are mature when they can handle life capably. Being exactly like Mom or Dad has little to do with it. They may be quite mature, just not like their parents. My children may be fully adult, even though they are not like me and never will be.

THREE OF FOUR FOLLOWED IN HIS FOOTSTEPS

Once there lived a great, white-haired grandfather. He was an avid goal setter and made a name for himself by his achievements. He was well known, respected, strong.

Three of his four children followed in his footsteps. They were aggressive, goal-setting leaders. One of his middle sons, however, was different. The grandfather had no appreciation, it seems, for his son's problem-solving genius. He viewed his son as passive and weak. The grandfather's disappointment in his youngest son was so deep that when the grandfather was interviewed for a story in the business section of a newspaper, he made no mention of him.

More interesting is how the dynamic plays out in the lives of that son's own children. They see and resent their grandfather's judgmental attitude. They see and regret their father's low self-esteem. And, subconsciously, they repeat the pattern. The grandchild who is a goal setter feels he's a winner. The grandchild who's a problem solver has low self-worth, and the grandfather's grievous error continues to live on.

Frequently, I hear this hurt-heart confession from men, "My dad never told me that he loved me, and he never told me that he was proud of me." What I hear from women at a similar emotional level is, "My mom won't let me grow up."

Some mothers assume that if they're problem solvers, their daughters should be problem oriented, or if they're goal setters, their daughters should be goal oriented, and that is how they will know their daughters are grown up. Such a mother might think, *I can tell my daughter she's a woman when she becomes like me, setting goals and taking responsibility.* But the daughter might be taking responsibility by solving problems, not by setting goals as her mother does.

Incidentally, I have come to define the starting point of manhood and womanhood as the time in life at which a respected adult of the same gender accepts us as equals. Then we feel we have passed into manhood or womanhood. That passage is rarely put into words: "You are a man now, my son" or "You are a woman now, my daughter." Instead, it is put into expressions such as, "I trust your judgment. You decide." Or "Come join our club." Or "You're quite a good person." When we sense that we have the acceptance of someone whose judgment we respect a great deal, we feel we've become an adult, even if our parents haven't had the eyes to see that we have or have not been available to help us through the passage.

If your parents have never seemed to understand you, perhaps they have never accepted your adulthood because your style is not like their style. One thing I discuss in my book *Why You Do What You Do* is calling your parents by their first names in your mind. When you see them in person, keep calling them Mom and Dad or whatever you call them. But mentally call them by their first names when you are thinking about them and asking yourself, "Why can't they accept the fact that I have grown up?"

Calling them by their first names does three things immediately:

1. It lets you look at them adult to adult instead of parent to child.
2. It adjusts your expectations of them. They have done, and are doing, the best they can.
3. It lets you see your parents as people, not just an image (*mom* or *dad* or *parents*).

Like many people, you might be able to understand your parents today better than they are able to understand you.

FREE ALL THOSE AROUND YOU
TO BE WHO THEY ARE

As I write this particular sentence, I'm sitting in the Admiral's Club at the Dallas–Fort Worth airport, just back from a trip to Japan and on my way to Dayton, Ohio, to be with my wife's parents and sister and our family for Thanksgiving. I am partly in jet lag, partly exhausted, partly rested, and partly excited.

As I sit here and teeter back and forth in this stuffed chair in the Admiral's Club, I want to share my favorite part of the Stop Setting Goals concept—the fact that it frees people to be who they are. We can free people by helping them to find where they fit, to understand why they don't fit, and to understand that it's okay to be different. It's okay to be a problem solver in a goal setter's world. It's okay to be a goal setter in a problem solver's world.

We live in a country where we should be free to be who we are. We should be free to be goal setters or problem solvers as we wish. For the most part, fortunately, we are.

Does the Stop Setting Goals idea make sense to you? Do you see the implications of helping people discover their natural strength areas and letting goal setters set goals and problem solvers solve problems?

If the Stop Setting Goals insight has helped you, may I suggest that you make it a lifelong mission—a magnificent obsession, as the movie called it—to free people to be who they really are?

It is my hope that, after reading this study of personal

assessment and team assessment, you will help all of the young people who look to you for leadership to understand what it means to be a round peg in a round hole and accept who they are. We should encourage them to accept who they are and where they are in terms of goal or problem orientation. We need to teach them to realize that both preferences are acceptable and neither is second class.

In the process of helping others, you might like to refer to the additional resources in the appendices. One thing I've spent a lifetime doing is developing materials that help people understand themselves better—why they do what they do, what their role preference is, why they are frustrated at work, and how to define their true *lifework*. Those things are often helpful to people in their lifelong pursuit of a round hole where they fit, where they belong, where they are a part, where they are a respected member of a team, and where they are a part of a whole.

Help adult members of your board, staff, or volunteer organization understand the implications of being either goal setters or problem solvers. Help them understand what naturally energizes them. Teach them how to work with people who are different from them. Help them see opposites as different but not less. Help them grow in their ability to develop a unified team to win their "championship."

Think of it as a secret mission to liberate the people you care deeply about, releasing them to realize their full potential in life and to become all that God intended them to be.

Appendix A

Accelerating the Problem-Solving Process: Brainstorming and Idea-Sorting Questions

The significant problems we face cannot be solved at the same level of thinking we were at when we created them.

—Albert Einstein

BRAINSTORMING CONDITIONS

Brainstorming is a highly effective technique for problem solving when:

- the information required to solve a problem is spread among several people,
- the implementation of the solution requires group acceptance,
- there is evidence that the results of brainstorming can be improved by techniques such as sequential (rather than random) contributions and by a personal-analogy technique in which one member of the group literally plays the part of the problem while the others question him or her.

Problem solving may often be done better by a single person. A group at Yale University demonstrated that individuals working alone could solve problems better than groups using the brainstorming process. Apparently, individuals examined *all* the alternatives, while teams tended to take a middle line. (The best answer does not always lie right down the middle.)[1]

BRAINSTORMING QUESTIONS TO HELP STRETCH AND ACCELERATE YOUR THINKING AS YOU REACH GOALS OR SOLVE PROBLEMS

Instructions

1. Before deciding on the *practicality* of an idea in a brainstorming session, get all of your ideas on the table by answering the Brainstorming Questions.

2. You may want to have the group respond after each suggestion—no matter how far-fetched—with a rousing, "Why not!"

3. After you have lots of fresh ideas on your list, begin sorting the good ideas from the great ones using the Idea Sorter List.

Brainstorming Questions

1. What is the one-word, one-sentence, or one-paragraph *essence* of our idea? Many words could be substituted for the word *idea,* such as, *program, project,* or *department.*

2. *Why* are we doing what we are doing?

3. What are our five most fundamental *assumptions?* List them in sequence from most important to least important.

4. What changes would we make if we had unlimited time to accomplish the task? What if we had three years? Three days? Three hours? Three minutes?

5. Where will this idea be ten, fifteen, twenty-five, fifty, one hundred, and five hundred years from now?

6. What would we accomplish if we had unlimited staff? Half the current staff? One or two extra people? What would they do? Why?

7. What changes would we make if we had double our current budget? Unlimited budget? Half the budget?

8. How can we double the income and cut our costs in half?

9. Which part of the total idea warrants extra funding?

10. Which part could we drop and not really miss?

11. What is the ultimate "blue-sky" potential of the idea?

12. What five things could keep us from realizing the full potential? How can we clear away those roadblocks?

13. What are our greatest strengths? How can we maximize them?

14. If we had to start over, what would we do differently?

15. What if this idea were one hundred times as successful as we plan?

16. What would it take to be number one in our entire field?

17. Where will our market be in fifty years?

18. What ten things do we want to accomplish in this area in the next fifty years?

19. How do we feel the environment will have changed for this idea in fifty years?

20. In our most idealistic dreams, where will our team be in fifty years?

NOTE: When considering alternative solutions, recognize that taking *no* action is an alternative and may even be the best choice. In that case, just recognize that the problem in question exists and deal with it on a day-to-day basis. That could be more practical than starting on an expensive program to eliminate the problem altogether.

IDEA SORTER LIST: QUESTIONS TO HELP YOU SORT YOUR GOOD IDEAS FROM YOUR GREAT IDEAS

1. Which idea best meets our needs (meets our design perimeters)?

2. Which has the most potential?

3. Which would be most cost effective in the long run?

4. Which best fits our overall master plan?

5. Which is most realistic for our staff and for our leader?

6. Which could help us win rather than just get by?

7. Which has the least front-end risk?

8. Which would work best day to day?

9. What facts do we need before we can properly decide?

10. Which is really worth the overall risk involved?

11. What are the predictable roadblocks?

12. How do our senior executive and board feel about the project?

13. Where would we get the funding to do it right?

14. Why have those who have tried similar ideas in the past failed?

15. What are the side effects—good and bad—of the idea we are considering?

16. Would I put my personal money into this project or idea?

17. Is the timing right?

18. Is it predictable, patentable, and copyrightable?

19. Would we have to stop something we are now doing to take on this project?

20. How can we test the idea before committing major resources to it?

Appendix B

Career Change Questions: Problem Solvers in a Goal Setter's World Or Goal Setters in a Problem Solver's World

NOTE: Not every question is expected to help in every situation. This is simply a checklist to help you keep from overlooking obvious questions. You will also want to add other questions that you find helpful in making career changes.

1. What are the major advantages of this career change? (Make a list.)

2. Why am I thinking of this change? What is my real motive?

3. What is the real price or loss of this change? (Make a list.)

4. What bones do I have to pick with my present employer? (Make a list.) Which ones might be eliminated if I talked with my boss?

5. Is this the right time for a move?

6. In my new position, do I want to put primary emphasis on the relationship I will have, the security the new position will bring, or the challenge of the position?

7. Where do I see myself in five to ten years? What is my overall career path? Does this change represent a step in the right direction in view of my long-range plans?

8. What do my three to five closest friends advise about the possible change? My spouse? My mentor?

9. What does my pastor say about the change?

10. How will the change affect:

   • my spiritual development?

   • my physical development?

   • my personal development?

- my family relationships?

- my social life?

- my professional life?

- my financial situation?

11. What would I do if I could do anything? If I had all of the time, money, education, and staff I needed; if God said He didn't care what I did; and if I knew I couldn't fail—what would I do?

12. If money were not an issue, would I still make this change?

13. If the doctor told me I had at most five years to live, what would I do then?

14. What needs do I see that make me want to weep? Make me want to explode with anger? Keep me awake at night? Should I do something about them in my next position?

15. What do I believe in enough to give my life for if necessary? In what ways can I work in support of that area?

16. What three to five things would I most like to do in my work? What do I feel best at and enjoy the most?

17. In what areas would I most like to grow personally and develop my full potential? Does this opportunity offer me the potential for growth in those areas?

18. What is really holding me back in my professional life? If I could overcome those obstacles, what would I do?

19. With whom would I most like to work (what person or persons)?

20. What would I like my epitaph to say? How would this career change affect the totality of my lifework?

21. If I had all of the skills to handle any position in the world, what position would I most like to have?

22. How much money would I like to make each year? Why?

23. At what age do I plan to retire? Why? What ten things do I want to do before then?

24. What accomplishments am I most proud of at this point in my life? Would those kinds of accomplishments be possible in my new position? Would I have more opportunities for such accomplishments or less?

25. Have I given myself at least twenty-four hours to pray and let this decision settle in my mind?

26. Are the pressure and tension of my present situation temporary or a constant, long-term problem?

27. Which position will make the most difference fifty years from now?

28. What questions are lingering in my mind that should be asked before I make a final decision?

29. What facts should I have before I make the final decision?

30. Do I have peace of mind about accepting or declining the opportunity as I pray about it and look at the decision from God's eternal perspective?

A FEW RULES OF THUMB TO CONSIDER WHEN MAKING A CAREER CHANGE

1. Be careful about the environment you choose; it will shape you.

2. Those individuals you work with might be more important than the company, the pay, or even the job.

3. Run *to* something, not *away* from something.

4. Life is too short to work at something you don't enjoy if you have a choice.

5. Choose work that lets you grow personally and become your best self, even though it may be a bit less secure.

6. Find work that lets you maximize your strengths and work on your weaknesses.

7. If you have an option, always choose a career where your work today will make a difference fifty years from now.

8. Every assignment you are given is preparing you for what God sees as your best possible position. Learn all you can as you go through an experience, and write it down so you will remember it well.

9. Work on meeting needs you feel emotional about.

10. God's timing is perfect.

Appendix C

Crisis Management and Damage Control: Preventing Problem Explosion

1. Pray and check our motives! Gaining God's perspective turns panicked minds to sovereignty.

2. Put the problem into big-picture context. Remember the positive progress we've already made.

3. Essence question: What is the situation?

4. Turn the sensational into simple truth. Answer falsehood or address the problem, and take positive initiative. Move from a defensive to a positive position. Talk about a positive future.

5. Remember, newspapers typically misquote. Love the people and assume positively.

6. Identify the legal implications. Be wise as a serpent and harmless as a dove.

7. Create a distribution list. Communicate simple honesty in love and concern for the well-being of everyone involved.

8. Identify the first three action steps.

9. Centralize the process of communication, if necessary.

10. Hold a question-and-answer session with the leadership team. Give an open and honest update, answer their anxiety questions, and ask for their support.

THINGS TO REMEMBER IN A CRISIS

1. People communicate sensationally in a crisis.

2. Newspapers sell sensation and fear.

3. What humans mean for harm, God means for good. Treat people in a Christian way, even in a crisis.

4. Focus on the question "What does this mean?"

5. Reduce the situation to the fewest number of working parts and concepts possible.

6. Assume we are making too much of the issue and, at the same time, that we are not making enough of the issue. It's dangerous to make either assumption completely, until the crisis is past.

7. Answer questions honestly or not at all!

8. Asking for help says, "We are on the same team."

Appendix D

Project Launch: Critical Questions to Help You Avoid Future Problems

1. What is the goal?

    a. Who is the intended audience?

    b. What demonstrated need is it filling?

    c. Is it consistent with our central mission?

    d. Is it duplicating another existing ministry or business?

    e. Is it compatible with our skills and experience, or is it a new type of endeavor for us?

2. What is the cost?

    a. How much new staff and space are required?

    b. Who has the time to manage it?

    c. How will this project impact the operations departments?

    d. What is the budget for the first two years?

    e. If it is funded by a grant, would we have done it without the grant?

    f. If the grant is terminated, will we continue the program?

3. How will we measure the success of this project?

    a. Will success meet the goal or solve the problem?

b. Will it pay for itself financially?

c. Will it generate new names for the mailing list?

d. What are the consequences if we terminate the program one year from now because it has not succeeded?

Appendix E

Proposal Analysis: Questions to Ask before You Agree to Take On a Project

As a leader, you will be brought many proposals (ideas, suggestions, plans, and the like) and will be asked to make a decision. That decision will involve hundreds, thousands, millions, or perhaps billions of dollars. Before you say yes to such a proposal, use these trouble spotting questions to identify potential roadblocks, land mines, splits, and clashes.

QUESTIONS TO ASK BEFORE YOU BEGIN

Here are some questions to ask yourself before you even begin to analyze a proposal. They'll help you make sure you are in a position to consider the proposal fairly and with a sense of balance.

There are four areas in which you'll want to do a self-check before even trying to make a wise decision by identifying the potential problems around the bend.

HEAD: How will this decision affect our master plan? My staff? My family? If necessary, what would I be willing to personally stop doing to take on this project?

HEART: Am I balanced spiritually today? Susceptible? Discouraged? Emotionally ragged?

HEALTH: Am I feeling well rested? In jet lag? Fatigued? Hyper?

STAFF: Who should be in the meeting and is not?

Once you determine that you are in a position to analyze the proposal fairly, ask the following questions:

1. Has the person making the proposal been briefed properly and the material screened (to keep from wasting my team's time)?

2. What person is key to the project's success or failure? Do I feel confident that this person can pull it off? How much time will he or she have to invest personally in the next twelve months?

3. Who will keep this from falling through the cracks?

4. What about royalties or other hidden or ongoing expenses?

5. How soon will we break even? Are the numbers realistic?

6. Are we planning to win big or get by?

7. What is our greatest possible loss if we don't go this way? What are our greatest benefits?

8. Where will we get the money?
   Raise $_____
   Borrow $_____
   Revolve $_____
   Staff/Time $_____
   When is it needed?

9. How do I see tying other parts of our organization to this project so that everyone wins?

10. What are the top three:

    - accelerators?
    - benefits?
    - critical moves?
    - land mines?
    - roadblocks?
    - probable misconceptions?
    - questions still in my mind?
    - tools?

11. Could I give a one-page summary of the proposal?

12. Is the timing right?

13. What are my lingering questions?

14. Why do I like this proposal personally?

Appendix F

Reporting on Priorities
(Goals or Problems)

When it comes to the subjects of establishing and supervising the implementation of priorities (goals or problems), one of the first questions that jumps to mind is, "What do I need to see to adequately track the priorities my staff sets?"

First of all, reporting assumes that you have measurable priorities upon which you and your staff have come to complete agreement. Once you have this agreement, there are only five questions that you really need to answer to keep abreast of the process of setting priorities and achieving them. This section will teach you not only what the questions are but also why they are so critical.

Second, reporting is something you should do whether or not you are asked by your team leader for a written report. Frequently, team leaders want information but are embarrassed to admit that they don't quite know how to ask for it. So they let the topic of written reporting slide along without ever really addressing it. Even if you are not asked, initiate in this area.

You may ask, "Why should I go to all of the trouble to ask for, or give, written reports?"

Over two thousand years ago, Jesus said, "The greatest among you will be your servant" (Matt. 23:11).

As a group leader, you are responsible to help your staff members achieve their goals. You are responsible to serve them by:

1. Giving them clear-cut decisions where needed.

2. Helping them remove the problems or roadblocks keeping them from their goals.

3. Helping them make realistic, well-thought-through, achievable plans.

4. Encouraging them as they pass key milestones.

5. Being aware of their personal lives so that you can stand with them in the low spots and celebrate with them when they are feeling on top of the world.

As a servant-leader, you serve those you lead in those ways.

A few years ago I asked Si Simonson, my colleague when I worked at World Vision and a world-class efficiency expert, "What is the most helpful question you know?" He hesitated approximately one inefficient millisecond and then nailed the heart of the issue with a simple but profound question, "What do you *have* to know to do what you *have* to do?"

As a servant-leader, what you need to know to do what you have to do, to serve your staff effectively, can be found in answering five simple reporting questions:

FIVE KEY REPORTING QUESTIONS

1. What *problems* do you need my help to solve?

2. What *decisions* do you need from me?

3. What *plans* are you making that we haven't discussed?

4. What *progress* have you made?

5. How are you doing *personally* on a scale of 1 to 100? Why?

If your staff members will answer these questions for you, you can help them reach their goals in ways that they have never before experienced. Having a simple report such as this has multiple advantages for you:

1. Clearer communications will occur (a major problem in most organizations).

2. Your staff members will clarify their thoughts by committing the answers to writing.

3. They have documentation of their progress and accomplishments.

4. You know clearly how to help them.

5. You have an effective method for telling your supervisors how they can best help your staff members.

6. You are never surprised.

7. You are available to your staff members and can help them in a focused, effective way.

8. By having the answers in writing, you reduce the miscommunication that often results from differing assumptions.

If you don't know what's going on with your staff, you can't help them reach their goals, and you can't serve them. Ultimately, you can't lead them.

A few questions are frequently asked as our staff discusses staff reporting:

QUESTIONS ABOUT WRITTEN REPORTING

1. How often should I have the staff report?

This depends on the organization. Some want to get this type of update weekly, some biweekly, and some monthly. The more complicated and nonroutine your organization is, the more often you will need to meet to keep abreast of the progress being made.

2. Should reports always be written, or can they be verbal in some cases?

For full-time staff, we recommend that reports always be written. For project leaders, volunteers, or part-time workers, reports can be verbal in some cases. Either way, you cover the same questions in the same order.

3. Why don't all organizations have reporting systems?
Some don't have goals against which to report. Others don't understand what to ask. Additionally, others seem to prefer to just drift along without seeming to care that a person is dying on the vine. Bottom line, they don't understand its importance.

4. What if some staff members don't turn in reports?
If you don't know what your staff members are doing, you can't help them. If they refuse to make it possible for you to help them by answering the five simple reporting questions once a week or so, you need to confront them on some issue.

5. What reaction can I expect when I introduce reporting?
Mixed. You will typically find that reactions fall into one of three categories:
   a. Relief and appreciation that you care—80 percent
   b. Fear of failure from a lack of confidence—15 percent
   c. Rebellion against any authority or structure—5 percent

6. How do staff meetings fit into reporting?
Look carefully, and you will see that the five reporting questions break into two types:
   a. Personal—better discussed one to one
   b. Public—better discussed in a group

   The personal questions include:
   a. decisions?
   b. problems?
   c. 1 to 100? Why?

   The group questions include:
   a. plans?
   b. progress?

7. Do I ever get to talk with my supervisor's supervisor?

Ideally, your supervisor will turn in copies of the staff members' reports with his or her reports to your supervisor's supervisor. If his or her supervisor needs or wants to know your perspective on an issue, that supervisor can always ask to get together with you personally or sit in on a board meeting, whichever the case may be.

The best way to talk with your supervisor's supervisor is typically just to ask your supervisor's permission. Never go around him or her without asking first.

Incidentally, what you need to see from your staff to serve them properly is exactly what the person responsible to help you win needs to see from you.

In conclusion, choose your staff members carefully. Help them define clearly where they want to go (goals), and then give them lots of encouragement, plus whatever clarification they need to grow into mature leaders.

Remember, someday your staff members will take your place when you move on. Your responsibility is to prepare them to be wise and caring servant-leaders.

NOTE: The senior executive's report to the board should cover the organizational master plan, the entire staff, and any problems anywhere in the organization requiring board attention.

TEAM REPORT

NAME_____ Date_____ 19___

TO REACH MY GOALS OR SOLVE MY PROBLEMS ON TIME . . .

1. I am having a problem with the following in achieving my priorities:

2. I need a decision from you on the following items to proceed toward my goals or solutions:

3. I am planning to:

4. I have made progress in the following areas: (include financial or numerical report here)

5. I would rate my personal happiness at _____ (1 = Suicidal and 100 = Best I've ever been) because:

NOTE: Feel free to adapt this form using your own letterhead.

Appendix G

Tackling the Impossible:
A Plan for Problems That Seem
Impossible to Solve

A few years ago, I was serving on a board with a prominent woman in Washington, D.C., and we discussed the fact that she had been asked to provide leadership for a national task force. That day on the plane ride home, I began asking myself what I would do if I were put in charge of the homeless situation or the drug war or given any assignment that was one hundred times larger than any I had ever encountered before. That's the day I developed the acrostic "A BAD CAM":

A—Assumptions

B—Basic problem
A—Alternatives
D—Decisions

C—Centenary view
A—Action
M—Momentum

To make it easy for you to use this process, I have turned the entire outline into a series of questions to ask whenever you are providing leadership for a problem that is ten to one hundred times larger than any you have ever encountered. I think the questions will provide you with a fresh and profound perspective and will help you to make the significant difference you are hoping to make.

A—ASSUMPTIONS

Assumptions are things we believe to be true. They are the basis on which we make our decisions and ultimately the basis on which we take all of the actions that we ever take in life. For a quick example, imagine you are driving down a road. You are assuming that when you reach a traffic light, red means stop, yellow means caution, and green means go.

You are approaching a traffic light, but because of fog in the region, you cannot tell whether the light is red, yellow, or green. Your assumptions might be clear, but if you can't make the proper distinctions, you don't know whether to stop, be cautious, or go. Once the fog clears and you determine that the traffic light is green (based on your assumption that green means go), you simply proceed through the intersection. Once you can determine the color of the light, it is easy to decide the appropriate action to take. Even though this is a simple illustration, it demonstrates the influence of assumptions on every part of our lives.

> **Problem solving is developing a life system based on faith rather than fear. A system that declares there is no problem too big . . . problems offer me an opportunity for growth . . . problems are always solvable. However, problem solving is not an easy fix but usually a change in life style.**
>
> —Claude Robold
> President of Mentoring Today

In taking on a megaproject, there are three fundamental assumptions that I would like to suggest to you in the form of questions.

1. Am I ready to commit ten to thirty years of my life to this project? Do I realize that I might not see signs of the major change I envision for at least ten years?

If you are not willing to commit a major amount of time to a major project, chances are you will just be frustrated with it. The adage "Rome was not built in a day" is far more than a cute saying from Roman history.

2. Do I have the amount of staff I need to carry it out? Am I willing to put together a staff of between three and three hundred thousand people to carry out this major assignment?

A word that I have used frequently in my consulting practice and that applies here is *capacity*. If you have three people to help you make the change you are wanting to make, you have the capacity of three people. But what if I were to give you the funding and equipment required to support thirty people? Or three hundred people? Or three thousand people? What capacity do you think you need to make the difference you want to make?

A lot of times, the real question in deciding to take on an assignment is, "Do we have the personnel capacity required?" Do we have the capacity, for example, to guard our borders or stop drug trafficking or revolutionize the educational system?

3. Do we have the required funds?

To make a significant difference, your project may require millions or billions of dollars. Is the party asking you to take on the assignment prepared to lay those kinds of dollars on the table?

Once you have gotten a commitment of the required time (years), energy (people), and funds (budget), then and only then are you really ready to consider taking on a problem ten to one hundred times the magnitude of any you have ever taken on.

B—BASIC PROBLEM

Charles F. Kettering is credited with first saying, "A problem well stated is a problem half solved." The fundamental question is, "What is the problem?"

One of my lifelong friends and frequent advisors, Bill Needham, says, "Contrary to frequently given management advice, don't start by defining the problem; start by defining the goal." A wise route toward problem resolution is to define the conditions or situations that should exist when a problem is solved. In the course of discussions it is important to recognize which phase you are in: goal definition, problem solving, or idea generation.

Your team moves toward problem resolution when it looks at the conditions that should exist when the problem is solved.

1. Am I trying to solve one problem at a time?

One of the most frustrating parts of defining a problem is complexity. Frequently, a multiplicity of intertwining problems is involved in any situation that you are trying to attack or approach. I encourage you to make a list of all the complications associated with the basic problem and get those on the table first, before you actually try to address the basic problem. For example, if you are attacking the problem of drug trafficking, your basic problem is drug trafficking, but supplemental issues might include education, law enforcement, court systems, and border patrol.

2. What trends, cycles, or changes in trends are affecting, accelerating, or even causing the problem you are working on?

Once I attended a conference of twenty-five presidents where the presenter for a three-day retreat was Peter F. Drucker, the world-renowned management guru. One of the points he made during our time together is that you should watch not only trends but also changes in trends. Be sure to ask yourself, "Is this a steady trend or has it changed substantially in the last few months, affecting our basic problem?"

3. What is the context of our basic problem?

By context, I mean something like a process chart, flow chart, or wiring diagram—a diagram like what you might see in the back of your television set. There might be only one bad piece in the whole television system, causing the whole system to go down, but unless you can understand the television wiring diagram, it is difficult to isolate that one component.

So ask yourself what the context of your basic problem is. What components led up to the problem and what components are implications of the problem? Once you find the "wiring diagram," it is much easier to determine the cause of the problem as well as the symptoms.

4. What research can help us distinguish between our facts and our faulty assumptions?

A high percentage of the time, I find that a little bit of research can make a world of difference in the clarity with which you are approaching a problem. Database decision making is a much more reliable part of the problem-solving process than going from assumption to assumption.

A—ALTERNATIVES

The underlying questions are these: What are our alternatives in terms of plans and actions? What are the possibilities in terms of solving the problem? Do we have several options?

1. Could brainstorming help create additional alternatives? (See Appendix A for stimulating brainstorming questions.)

2. What have other people already tried?

Frequently, a review of what other people have tried unsuccessfully uncovers possibilities that you have not considered. Even though others failed in their attempts, you might find that you can solve problems that stumped your predecessors. What didn't work for them may work for you.

3. What models are working in other areas that might be adaptable to ours?

In your research, you might find that others in another country, state, or region are doing something similar to what you are trying to do. By taking a trip to see what they are doing, you might find a viable alternative model already in place that is easily adaptable and expandable to your needs.

D—DECISIONS

Once you have several alternative courses of action, you need to make some decisions. You need to decide how to assign and prioritize your time, energy, and money.

1. What are the relevant facts?

One of the principles of life that Peter Drucker teaches is, "Once the facts are clear, the decisions jump out at you." It is important to have the facts associated with the three to five fundamental decisions you have to make.

2. With which existing groups, networks, or distribution channels can we work in order to maximize our cooperative relationships with other people and to maximize their strength as well as our own?

A fundamental part of making a major change is networking with other organizations or groups who have complementary and additional resources that would help solve the problem that you are working on.

3. Who are the ten key influences or gatekeepers affecting this decision?

On any major problem you ever work with, no matter how large, if you can affect the thinking and actions of the ten most influential individuals in the area, you can move toward solving the problem and increase the speed with which you solve the problem. These individuals are the gatekeepers of the information, staff, time, energy, and money needed to solve the problem.

C—CENTENARY VIEW

Another fundamental dimension is a centenary view of each of the alternatives. What I mean by a *centenary view* is a hundred-year look, a big-picture perspective, a macro look at each leg of your plan. For example, if you were the drug czar, you'd take a hundred-year look at drug education, border control, and so forth. You would ask yourself, "What fundamental things can we put in place in the next year to ten years that will last for fifty to a hundred years? How can we rewrite the history of drug control for the next hundred years?"

When you are taking the centenary view, you can consider at least four dimensions:

- Strategy, which is how you will get things done.
- Spirit, which is the morale, energy, and excitement of getting things done.
- Systems, which are the basic and fundamental resources required to get things done.
- Specifics, which are the myriad things that must and should be done.

We will start with strategies. What will be our strategy for accomplishing our goal or for solving our problem?

Strategies

1. Can we come up with a totally new idea that will solve the problem?

As I mentioned in the Role Preference Inventory, a certain percentage of the people in any group prefer starting with a blank sheet of paper and coming up with original alternatives or original strategies to solve any problem.

When I am working with a group, I like to identify those people who are the designers and designer-developers by role preference. I then present them with the problem and ask them to come up with a wide variety of totally original solutions. Watching them create new solutions is instructive. Look for the designers and designer-developers on your team to brainstorm original solutions.

2. What can we accomplish in the first one hundred days?

A key insight of most new presidents of countries as well as corporations over the years is that the first hundred days in office are critical in shaping the acceptance, policies, goals, and priorities of the new administration. Think carefully about each of the offensive centenary strategies you want to put together. During your first one hundred days, make sure that you launch the primary facets of your project properly because the first one hundred days of going public will be very important to you.

3. How can we most effectively cut off the problem at its source?

Try to identify the source or cause of the problem—the chief fuel supply for the problem—and cut it off. For example, if you were the drug czar, how would you cut off the supply of drugs into the country at its source?

4. What kind of team do we need in place to carry out our plans?

Teams can be boards we establish, task forces we appoint, consultants we retain, and so forth. But which team can actually carry out our strategies?

5. How many foot soldiers do we really need?

If the problem you are working on is large enough, you might need thirty to three hundred thousand people helping you solve the problem. Make absolutely sure that you have adequate supplies of people with the specific talents necessary to help you.

Incidentally, I have found that probably the greatest single distinction between presidents who can build firms effectively and those who cannot is whether or not they know how to organize their staff via organizational charts. Organizational charts and position descriptions are indispensable.

6. What model has been most successful in the past?

In planning a strategy to solve major problems, it is important to scour the universe to find parallel models, models of how other people have done it successfully in other parts of the world.

In some situations you cannot find an exact model, but you can find a comparable model in another field. If you can find a model that is actually working and adapt it, typically it will save you hundreds or even thousands of hours and potentially millions of dollars on a major project.

Once you have developed a prototype of how you plan to do it, and that becomes a model that can be duplicated, you are ready to roll out. For example, if you are attacking the problem of homelessness, you might look at an organization such as the Union Rescue Mission in downtown Los Angeles to find out what they have actually been doing with the homeless for more than a hundred years. Any model with a long and successful history can be adapted for use in similar situations around the country. It is always easier to work with what is already working and to move with what is already moving.

7. How can we mobilize volunteers to help?

Obviously one of the most fundamental natural resources in any culture is the people who will give freely of their time as volunteers. In working on a major problem, you need grassroots involvement and training programs, training materials, and volunteer captains to mobilize all the volunteers you can possibly mobilize to help solve the problem.

Diagnostic Questions

8. What three critical steps can we take in solving each facet of the problem?

If you could make only three critical moves in each dimension of the problem that would make a 50 percent difference, what would they be? For example, again, if you were the drug czar, what three critical steps could you take in drug education, border patrol, law enforcement, and court systems.

9. What is the "rocket"?

Is there one idea anywhere in all your brainstorming that is so powerful it could successfully launch the entire project? Identify, isolate, study, and develop this program or idea. It is your *rocket*. Put all the time, energy, and money necessary on this single idea and launch it strongly so that the program has the finest chance of being successful.

10. What cycles can we take advantage of?

Just as there are cycles in the problem, so also there are cycles in the solution. What is the best time of year to launch a major answer to the problem?

11. What laws might have to be changed?

Occasionally, there is poorly written or outdated legislation against the progress you wish to make. You might actually have to get the law changed to allow the problem to be solved.

Changes in Spirit

12. What would happen if we developed a first-class, top-drawer, top-cotton image of the program we have in mind?

What should be the image of our program? I find it helpful to compare the image to an automobile. If you say, for example, that we want our image to be like a Rolls Royce, a Corvette convertible, a Buick Roadmaster Sedan, a 1969 Volkswagen Beetle, or a two-year-old Lexus, your group will identify the image pretty quickly.

13. If we stretch our moral imagination, what do we see?

What moral codes have been violated? What is the high ground, the most profound look at what is true, right, noble, just, and righteous? Study these as a solution to the problem.

14. How can we stay positive in the middle of the program?

What does our staff need to keep a positive attitude, a positive focus, a progress-and-results focus instead of a distance-to-go focus?

15. What is our dream?

Bill Bright, founder and president of Campus Crusade for Christ, an organization that has more than 40,000 staff members in more than 150 countries, says, "Small dreams do not inflame the minds of men." What dream of solving the problem is so grand that it energizes the minds and hearts of all the volunteers and paid staff you've got working on the problem?

16. How do we restore a hope of winning?

One reality is that people lose hope. When team members lose hope, they become discouraged. When you restore hope, they become encouraged. What can we do to restore hope that the problem is, in fact, solvable?

One simple but important encouragement, I've found, is reporting results. In the beginning this will include every tiny step of progress. By reporting results, you portray each small advance as the major victory that it is. Keep reporting results, and you will find morale staying high.

Systems

17. What training and literature do we need to keep the problem's solution ever before the people involved?

One time I asked the leader of a major movement, "What are the keys to keeping a movement alive?" His answer was that you need to control two things: the training and the literature. How will the training program and the literature affect your problem solution?

18. How will we develop the ongoing funding necessary to keep the solution in place?

You can solve the problem temporarily and have it come back stronger than ever if you don't have the funding to keep the solution in place.

19. What equipment do we need in place?

Computers, faxes, telephones, machinery—such things are powerful tools for solving many problems.

20. If all of this information seems unwieldy right now, remember that there are essentially only four systems that need to be in place for a healthy, functioning organization:

- Resources: This means developing resources (primarily people and money) for their most efficient use within your organization.
- Operations: This is everything from accounting and personnel to maintenance.
- Services: This is an actual service or product that is provided to the public.
- Feedback: This includes all communication systems up and down the line—from resources to operations to services and back.

There needs to be a balance between the resources, operations, services, and feedback as well as systems linkage among the four systems.

Specifics

21. What tools do we really need to solve this problem?

A friend and client came to me one day and wrote a formula on a piece of paper. It said: MMW = HR × Tools. He explained that the formula means, "Man's Material Welfare equals Human Resources times Tools."

My friend added this illustration: If you are a laborer in South America in a jungle filled with mahogany trees, your material welfare will equal human resources, which in this case is one person, times tools. Let's say you have one saw, and the mill for the mahogany trees is thirty miles away. In one year, you could probably cut down enough mahogany trees with that one saw and carry enough lumber to the mill thirty miles away through the jungle to make one hundred dollars. Therefore, in the example, man's material welfare is one hundred dollars a year.

Now, let's add some tools. You're still one laborer in a jungle with unlimited natural resources, the vast supply of mahogany trees. But this time you have two or three chain saws, a front-end loader, and a truck. We've added just a few tools, but now you could get three or four logs to the mill per day. At the end of the year, you would have made thirty thousand to fifty thousand dollars. Therefore, man's material welfare with the addition of a few tools is several hundred times what it is without those tools.

The formula is crude, of course, but it illustrates clearly the power of the right tools. When properly applied, the right tools will help you reach your goal or solve the problems your team is attacking.

A—ACTION

1. What myths need to be exposed?

A crucial educational device in solving a major societal or system problem is to expose the myths that grow up around the problem. For example, as the drug czar, you might expose the myth that drug lords live in impenetrable fortresses in the jungle and cannot be attacked successfully. Anything you can do to destroy that myth will help in solving the drug problem.

2. Who will be our driving force?

Who should be the driving force for each of the sub-projects? To solve each aspect of a major problem, you must assign to it the person with the appropriate energy, ability, and wisdom. The person will be the driving force in making sure that a solution is found. Who are the people with a sense of dynamic drive to carry each solution to completion?

3. What capacity do we need?

Focus on creating capacity: people capacity, money capacity, and systems capacity. Do not deal with just one person, one county, one state, or one province but with all of the people, counties, states, and provinces that are affected by the problem you are trying to solve.

4. What three things can we do in the next ninety days to make a 50 percent difference?

You encountered this question earlier in the book, but it is a powerful question in focusing priorities, be they goals or problems. Take each of the major sections of the solution and ask the question. What three educational things can we do in the next ninety days to make a

50 percent difference? What three systems priorities can we put in place in the next ninety days to make a 50 percent difference? What three personnel appointments can we make in the next ninety days to make a 50 percent difference? And so on throughout the project.

M—MOMENTUM

1. What results have we seen?

As I said earlier, nothing motivates like results. Establish communication links with the people who are trying to help you solve the problem.

2. What progress have we made?

You might not have seen a lot of results yet, but you have made progress. If you are opening a restaurant that is far bigger than any you've opened before, you might not have sold a hamburger yet, but you've made progress in getting the stoves in place, the carpet laid, and so forth. Whenever you're in the middle of a project and someone asks how things are going, one of the most encouraging responses you can make is, "We are making excellent progress in the process!"

3. What is working?

One feature in the literature you put out on a regular basis to the people involved in the process might be called "IT'S WORKING!" This is a feature space in which you applaud anything that is currently working or winning. Applaud anything that has the air of exciting, positive progress or results. Call attention to any model that's working, anything that's really making a difference.

4. Are we recognizing people (especially volunteers) and meeting their needs to help them maintain their momentum?

When I wrote the book *Why You Do What You Do*, I discovered eight needs that volunteers have, eight needs that people in general have. If your team is not meeting the personal needs of volunteers and staff

members, sooner or later your momentum will really begin to deterio-
rate. The eight needs from *Why You Do What You Do* are:

1. The need to be loved *without conditions.*
2. The need to make a *significant difference.*
3. The need to be *admired* as a hero.
4. The need to be *recognized* as an individual.
5. The need to be *appreciated* for a job well done.
6. The need to be *secure.*
7. The need to be *respected* as an equal.
8. The need to be *accepted* by the group.

If you will continue to meet the appropriate need in each person in
one of those eight areas, momentum will be sustained. If you neglect
the needs, motivation, momentum, and morale will begin to sag.

5. What media systems do we have in place to consistently communicate our message?

I serve on the board of directors of a major media organization
whose radio program is broadcast ten thousand times a week. As a
result, many people who are trying to be a part of the solution that
organization is seeking get encouragement, instruction, information,
and inspiration. They remain connected to the priorities, dreams,
hopes, accomplishments, and plans of the organization. What media
vehicles could you use to keep in touch with those who are faithfully
serving as a part of your solution process?

6. Where are we succeeding?

One thing I've seen demonstrated over and over is that the expression "nothing succeeds like success" is right on target. When your
team succeeds in solving even minor problems, and that success is
recognized in a visible way, the people working on solutions are encouraged, which begets even more enthusiasm, belief, and momentum. People begin to say, "If that community can prevent five kids
from experimenting with drugs, our community can do it as well."
Success begets success. Results beget results. Encouragement begets
encouragement. Hope begets hope.
  Whenever you face a problem that is ten to one hundred times larger

than any you have faced before—when the odds seem overwhelming and the possibility of success seems slight—and you are the leader, the one charged with finding a solution, don't ever forget "A BAD CAM":

A—Check your *assumptions*.

B—Define your *basic problem*.
A—Come up with *alternative approaches*.
D—*Decide* which alternatives are the most reasonable.

C—Take a *centenary view* of how to implement.
A—Take *action*.
M—Keep the *momentum* going for a long time.

Appendix H

Team Discussion Questions to Maximize the Value of This Book

Following are a few discussion questions to help your team explore the implications of the Stop Setting Goals model for your team or organization.

1. Am I a goal setter or a problem solver?

2. Have I found my energy different when I work consistently in my preferred area—goal setting or problem solving? How does it affect my natural energy level?

3. How many dollars' difference would it make in a year if we let goal setters set goals and problem solvers define their work in terms of problems and we all worked together as a team?

4. What pressures are on me to be who I am not? Am I a goal setter in a problem solver's world or a problem solver in a goal setter's

world? Or am I a goal setter in a goal setter's world or a problem solver in a problem solver's world?

5. What does the statement "everyone is not like me" mean to me?

6. Do I feel emotional about goal setting and problem solving? If so, how?

7. What percentage of the people within a hundred miles of where we are sitting prefer solving problems to setting goals?

8. How do I orient myself over a year's time? Over the last twelve months, how have I oriented myself? By keeping a list of goals I have set and am reaching or a list of problems I am solving? Neither? Both?

9. Do I really feel our organization can come to the place where goal setting and problem solving are not seen as good or bad, but just different?

10. Am I convinced of the significance of my fourth-grade experience? What did I learn about myself by thinking back to fourth grade?

11. Do I identify with the comment that goal setters tend to look down on problem solvers and problem solvers also tend to look down on goal setters?

12. How can our team dream be large enough to unify us as goal setters and problem solvers?

13. Is our team problem oriented or goal oriented at this point? Which would I like us to be?

14. If I were to guess what each member of our team prefers, which members would I guess are problem oriented and which would I guess are goal oriented?

15. What keys to relating to and maximizing goal setters and relating to and maximizing problem solvers have I learned?

16. Do I give my family and friends the freedom to be who they are without expecting them to become more like me?

17. Can I see myself helping people be who they are and fill the niche that fits them?

18. Of those listed in this book, which benefits would most affect our team if we adopted the Stop Setting Goals model on our team?

19. What is the most obvious violation of the round-pegs-in-round-holes philosophy I've ever seen?

20. Have I ever felt like a second-class citizen? How did it feel? Do I still feel that way after reading this material? If not, how does it feel to no longer feel like a second-class citizen?

21. What is our team's dream and primary result?

22. If we could solve only three problems or reach only three goals in the next ninety days that would make a 50 percent difference in where we'll be at the end of the year, what would they be?

23. Would I describe our corporate culture as a goal-setting culture or a problem-solving culture?

24. What role did I play in the fourth grade, and how does it affect my adult leadership?

25. At what point could we switch to being a totally problem-oriented organization instead of a goal-oriented organization? Should we?

26. What is the key to presenting a good idea to me? What needs to be a part of the process to make sure that I am open to the new idea?

27. What is the key to talking with me about problems in our organization without draining me?

Appendix I

Additional Resources to Maximize Both Problem Solvers and Goal Setters

Asking to Win!

This booklet (part of Masterplanning Group's Pocket Confidence series) fits in your suitcoat pocket, briefcase, or purse. It contains one hundred profound questions, ten for each of the following situations:

1. *Avoiding*: small talk.
2. *Balancing*: life's priorities.
3. *Brainstorming*: to maximize your finest ideas!
4. *Career-ing*: when you or a friend is considering changing careers.
5. *Deciding*: when you need to make a risky, pressurized, costly decision.
6. *Interviewing*: getting behind the smile of a potential team member.
7. *Focusing*: putting your life into focus or refocusing.
8. *Organizing*: your life to maximize your time.
9. *Parenting*: to keep children growing.
10. *Solving*: any problem faster.

Whenever you face a tough situation, ask profound questions to get profound answers and make wise decisions. The booklets in this series are packaged and priced reasonably so that you can give them to adult children, colleagues, friends, protégés, spouses, and staff members.

Focusing Your Life
Often life, even for a leader, gets foggy, confused, and overwhelming. *Focusing Your Life* simplifies life!

Focusing Your Life is a simple, step-by-step process that you can learn in about three hours. It helps clear the fog and keeps you feeling focused for the rest of your life.

Focusing Your Life has been used by more than four thousand people to help form a crystal-clear direction in life. The program contains an outline (three-ring notebook) and three audio cassettes.

Leadership Confidence
Approximately 3,500 people have completed the *Leadership Confidence* series. This series is a lifelong reference covering thirty essential leadership areas including:

How to cope with:
    change
    depression
    failure
    fatigue
    pressure

How to become more:
    attractive
    balanced
    confident
    creative
    disciplined
    motivated

How to develop skills in:
    asking
    dreaming
    goal setting
    prioritizing
    risk taking
    influencing
    money management
    personal organization
    decision making

problem solving
communicating

How to become more effective in:
delegating
firing
reporting
motivating
people building
recruiting
masterplanning
team building

Leadership Confidence comes in two formats:

1. A 225-page paperback book
2. A 166-page outline in a three-ring binder with eight hours of drive-time audiocassette tapes

Process Charting: How to Do It!
Process charting is possibly the most valuable and least understood leadership skill.

A clear understanding of process charting provides a framework for fundamental organizational components such as: policy, procedure, problem solving, predicting impact, staff communications, curriculum development, logic checking, filing, monitoring, program overview, program transfer, new staff orientation, and time lines.

Understanding process charting is also key to quality control and transferability. Contains a three-ring notebook and audiocassette tapes.

Role Preference Inventory
The *Role Preference Inventory* is a proven (sixth edition, seventeenth printing since 1980) way of understanding yourself better.

In simple language, it lets you tell your spouse, your friends, or your colleagues what makes you tick, what turns you on, and what burns you out!

The *Role Preference Inventory* helps you distinguish what you really want to do, what you have to do, what you have done the most, or what you think others expect of you. It is the key to understanding personal fulfillment and is an affordable way of building strong team unity by predicting team chemistry.

This simple, self-scoring, self-interpreting inventory is the key to selecting the right person for the position, thus helping you avoid costly hiring mistakes. One inventory per person.

Senior Executive Profile

- Am I cut out to be a president, senior pastor, or head coach?
- Where do I need to grow to be ready when the opportunity comes to be a senior executive?
- Which of the candidates we are interviewing for the senior executive position rates highest on the Senior Executive Profile?
- What dimensions do I look at to evaluate (on a one-to-ten scale) our current senior executive?

If you have been asking yourself any of those questions, you need this easy-to-understand profile. It is a proven guide for individual reflection and team discussion or evaluation. The *Senior Executive Profile* helps you identify, evaluate, define, and understand.

Strategy Work Sheets
A quick, systematic, step-by-step method for thinking through a solid success strategy for each of your goals.

Use these 11″ × 17″ sheets to help each staff member to draft strategies for turning major goals into realistic plans.

Strategy Work Sheets help you spot problems in basic thinking and strategy before they become costly. Includes twenty-four sheets for use with your team.

The Question Book
Decisions, decisions, decisions! Ninety-nine experts offer twenty questions to ask before making particularly stressful decisions in their specialty areas.

The Question Book is a lifelong reference book. Topics are arranged alphabetically for easy access. It's an ideal resource for people who live alone and need to test their thinking to gain a more objective perspective before making any decision—*especially* if a former wise adviser is no longer available for counsel.

The Question Book makes a great gift from a parent to an adult child. It supplements experience and wisdom without making the parent appear nosy or domineering. The questions reduce the stress of making a risky decision in a field in which you have little or no experience.

Buy a copy for each staff member and save your team thousands of dollars by enabling team members to make wise decisions.

To receive free information on:

- Bobb Biehl's speaking schedule
- Consulting by the Masterplanning Group

Call (407) 333-9716.

Or write:

Masterplanning Group
Box 952499
Lake Mary, Florida 32795

To order any of the resources listed or to receive a copy of Master-planning Group's complete resource catalogue, call:

(800) 969-1976.

Notes

Introduction

1. Stephen R. Covey, *The Seven Habits of Highly Effective People: Restoring the Character Ethic* (New York City: Simon & Schuster, 1989), 75.

Chapter 3

1. *Business Week,* July 26, 1993.

2. D. M. Hall, *Management of Human Systems* (Cleveland: Association for Systems Management, 1971).

Chapter 4

1. Mary Kay Ash, *Mary Kay on People Management* (New York: Warner Books, 1984).

Chapter 5

1. Ron Zemke with Dick Schaaf, *The Service Edge* (New York City: New American Library, 1989), 67.

2. Ibid., 405.

3. Ibid., 454.

4. Ibid., 507.

5. Jerre L. Stead, "Tap your people's power: U.S. business needs greater employee involvement," *Industry Week,* April 2, 1990, 32. (Copyright 1990 by Penton Publishing, Inc.)

6. Joseph and Suzy Fucini, *Entrepreneurs: The Men and Women Behind Famous Brand Names and How They Made It* (Boston: G. K. Hall & Co., 1985), 113–15.

7. Andrew Erdman, "Companies That Train Best," *Fortune,* March 22, 1993, 62*ff.*

8. "Constant improvement is key to compete" (Alfred P. Sloan Foundation president Ralph Gomory's speech at the Economic Growth and the Commercialization of New Technologies Conference), *Tooling & Production,* December 1989, 6. Copyright 1989 by International Thomson Industrial Press, Inc.

Chapter 6

1. Scott DeGarmo, "Creative attack! No joke—here's how to get the jump on the competition," *Success,* June, 1990, 4. (Copyright 1990 by Lang Communications.)

Chapter 7

1. "Alfred Sloan, Move Over," *Chief Executive*, July/August 1993.

2. Magaly Olivero, "Get crazy! How to have a breakthrough idea," *Working Woman,* September 1990, 144. Copyright 1990 by Working Woman-McCall's Group.

3. Joseph and Suzy Fucini, *Entrepreneurs: The Men and Women Behind Famous Brand Names and How They Made It,* (Boston: G. K. Hall & Co., 1985), 111–13.

Appendix A

1. Thomas J. Bouchard, "When to Use Brainstorming as a Problem Solving Technique," *Industry Week,* August 2, 1971, 26.

LINCOLN C   GE AND SEMINARY

658.3
B5868

11233

LINCOLN CHRISTIAN COLLEGE AND SEMINARY

3 4711 00176 6593